Memoir of a Miracle

(Journey of Faith)

If you want to know love, love another
If you want to know God's love, love another
If you want to know <u>how</u> to love God, love
someone who does not love you!

Dawn Curazzato & Ladies of the Lord

Memoir of a Miracle

(Journey of Faith)

Dawn Curazzato

Lightning Source

ISBN
0-9726183-0-9

Library of Congress Cataloging in Publication Data
00-111746

Dawn Curazzato
Memoir of a Miracle

10 9 8 7 6 5 4 3 2 1

Kolbemax Press
162 Sundown Trail
Williamsville, NY 14221

This book is dedicated to

Katelin McQuaid and Audrey Santo

Through their suffering many have been made aware of the sanctity of life and have renewed their relationship with Jesus Christ

&
Ginger Faley

This is a special dedication to my mother who is battling cancer. Her love, sacrifice, generosity and encouragement exemplify motherhood. She was there to pick me up the first time I fell. She is there for me still. Mom, I love you. May this book honor you for the blessing you are and may the Good Lord bless you with a healing.

Forward

*T*hroughout history, the miraculous has been the object of both intense belief and deep cynicism. We in the Western Hemisphere, so influenced by the Enlightenment and impressed by modern technology and the social sciences, seem particularly reluctant to take anything 'on faith'. As Americans, we all seem to be from Missouri, " *the show me state,*" when it comes to alleged stories of Eucharistic Miracles or Marian apparitions. And yet, underneath this skepticism is a deep desire for the transcendent, which I think, is easily overlooked – even by pious believers. One only need turn on the television to see this respect for the supernatural taking various forms, everything from *"Psychic Friends,"* to *"Unsolved Mysteries,"* to *"Buffy, the Vampire Slayer."* St. Paul was similarly impressed with the ancient Greek culture. Were he able to channel surf even briefly, he might say to we Missourians what he said so long ago to the ancient Athenians, *"I see how extremely religious you are in every way. For as I went through the city and looked carefully at the objects of your worship, I found among them an altar with the inscription 'To an unknown god.' What therefore you worship as unknown, this I proclaim to you! The God who made the world and everything in it ...made all the nations to inhabit the whole earth...so that they would search for God and perhaps grope for him and find him... for 'in him we live, and move and have our being' as even some of your own poets have said."* (Acts of the Apostles 17:22-28). While St. Paul may have been as privately repulsed by the Greek pantheon of gods as we might be at roadside signs for psychics, spiritualists or palm-readers, his genius is that he affirms the basic desire for spirituality among this people. He starts with the good; the human desire (however misguided or mistaken) for God.

What has surprised me the most about my experiences with Dawn and her family is the immediate response of my brother priests. Men I know and love personally and respect as compassionate and competent priests are quite put off by these wonderful, miraculous experiences. Their first and sometimes ongoing reaction is one of great doubt and reservation. Unlike St. Paul they do not affirm the good faith that has brought these earnest people to renewed faith and propelled them into active service. Even the more welcoming—-including myself—-are careful to exhort them about "private and public revelation" and caution them not to get too carried away. Some men who every day preach the mysteries of the resurrection, ascension, transfiguration, pentecost, trinity, the virgin birth, the multiplication of loaves, the miraculous healings of Christ and the miracle of the Eucharist itself, seem completely unable to affirm the experiences of dear and honest people like Dawn even on a non-official personal level.

If there is one thing my discoveries of Marian spirituality, Charismatic prayer and Eucharistic adoration have shown me is how little we trust in the awesome promises of God. Dawn and others like her have shown to me in a very real, experiential way, the sweetness and joy of the faith; without which it can become mere law and duty and obligation. It has also revealed a great divide in our church, which makes me fear for our future. I appeal to my brother-priests; should we not affirm the earnest faith of these sincere people, correct what (if anything) is in error and assist them in their spirituality rather than dismissing them as "miracle-people". I affirm, along with the Second Vatican Council that *"those who have charge over the church should judge the genuineness and proper use of these gifts, through their office not indeed to extinguish the Spirit but to test all things and hold fast to what is good* (Dogmatic Constitution of the Church, *Lumen Gentium*, 12). Perhaps we would serve the church more effectively if we saw them as people with a special gift or vocation; one we might not share, understand or even accept as genuine; yet one that deserves the charity we would offer anyone, even the least of the brothers or sisters.

The truth is these folks challenge us but this is why God has placed them in our lives! Let us be patient then, affirming their zeal and not simply dismissing them in the name of "balance." After all, demanding 'balance" from a person with a prophetic or charismatic gift is like Our Lord, Jesus demanding that John the Baptist lower his voice and avoid eating so many grasshoppers! Let us therefore keep an open mind, test the spirits and act toward all with the love and tenderness of Christ.

Rev. Edward "Ted' Jost
St Christopher R.C. Church
Tonawanda, New York

Table of Contents

Forward: Rev. Edward Jost
i

Preface: Rev. Msgr. Richard T. Nugent & Rev. James Ciupek
ix

Special Acknowledgement: Dawn Curazzato
xiii

Introduction: Dawn Curazzato
xv

CHAPTERS

Mike Wachowicz 1

Medjugorje 5

Lisa 6

Joe 8

Shane 13

Katelin 13

Homecoming 19

Faith 22

Suffering 25

My Gethsemane 27

The Dominican and Carmelite nuns 29

The Healing Mass 31

Family Ties 34

Audrey Santo 37

The Trip 40

Home 46

The Baptism 64

More Suffering 68

Tests and a Touch of Heaven 71

Friendship and Humor 74

Confession 80

Priests are People Too 84

Troubled Waters 87

A Chance to Help 89

The Real Presence 91

A Step out in Faith 94

The Second Trip 97

Channel 7 News Special 101

More Gifts 104

Mission 106

The Ladies of the Lord 108

"By Their Fruits You Shall Know Them" 112

Science and Miracles 114

Proof? 117

Motherhood, Abortion and God 120

Connor, Katelin and God 124

Epilogue 126

Poems and Letters 128

Preface

My initial meeting with Dawn Curazzato several years ago was memorable, since she came "bearing gifts"— not only of sweet rolls and cakes — but of an open faith and trust in Jesus and His Mother Mary. She was on a mission of mercy for her granddaughter, Katelin who needed a physical miracle to survive in this world. She found her answer and her miracle in another child – a victim-soul, Audrey Santo, in Worcester, Massachusetts. Today, her granddaughter lives a normal life — but not without some difficulty. Dawn, however, continues her life of faith and trust that all will work out — so long as prayer remains central in her life. Meantime, the "gifts" precede her — as she brings her message of faith and trust in God and His Mother to anyone who will listen and be open. Those who remain closed to her message of mercy will simply take a little more time, prayer and patience.

Rev. Msgr. Richard T. Nugent
Pastor St Bernadette R.C. Church
Orchard Park, N.Y. 14127

A story of Faith… A story of Love… Dawn has given us both in what follows. I suppose most of us, at one time or another, search for answers and meaning to our lives, especially when confronted with difficult experiences. The modern-day world wants to provide us with answers to all of our problems, but we know that such responses are painfully inadequate when applied to suffering and loss. In a straightforward manner, Dawn shares with us a part of her personal journey of faith – a journey which has taken her through some very difficult moments, but which also has graced her with some deep spiritual experiences. Ultimately, Dawn shows us that there is something "more" to life than the world-at-large tends to offer - and that is the place, which God has in our lives. Truly inspirational! Dawn's commitment to what she believes has been an example to me in my own faith life as a priest. Interwoven throughout is the overwhelming sense of love, which Dawn has for God, her family, and the people whose lives she touches. Without reservation, Dawn reminds us all of where our priorities need to be. Open your heart and let the Holy Spirit speak to you in this remarkable story.

Rev. James D. Ciupek
St Peter and Paul R.C. Church
Hamburg, New York

Special Acknowledgement

$\mathcal{I}$ thank my spiritual advisor Msgr. Richard Nugent who encouraged me to write this book and who is an inspiration to me. I also thank my spiritual friend Maximillion Kolbe.

My gratitude to my loving husband Sam, my son Joe and my courageous daughter Lisa, who are my source of strength and love, as are Pat, Shane, Katelin and Conner. You are all my reason for living.

To my dad for his Irish humor and his strong faith which will live on through all of us.

To Father Jim Ciupek, Father Ted Jost, Father Richard DiGiulio, Msgr. David Lee, the Dominican and Carmelite nuns and all the priests and nuns who have affected my life in a positive manner. Your dedication to spreading the love of Christ throughout the world is the saving grace to all of us who live in it.

To Mike Wachowicz and his family.

To the "Ladies of the Lord" who are so special to me: Thank you, Mary, Linda, Kathy, Lucy, Donna, Maria, Peggy, Delores, Mary Clair, Mary, Paula and Ivanka.

With special thanks to Mary and Bob Roth whose help made this book possible. They compensated for my computer illiteracy and Bob saw to it that every necessary piece of computer software was at my fingertips and when my "fingertips" made mistakes, Mary did the cleanup! I love you and thank you.

Most importantly, I thank God, the Blessed Mother and all the angels and saints who were at my side through every step of my "journey of Faith. May this story give glory and honor to Our Lord Jesus Christ.

Introduction

$\mathcal{O}$n a recent visit to the Carmelite Monastery one of the externals (cloistered nuns who move about and are allowed to speak to the laity) stopped me and said, "I see you here very often. What is your name, dear?'

"Dawn, Sister." I answered.

The little nun was quite bent over due to arthritis no doubt. Upon hearing my name she recoiled and forced her head back to look up at me. In a stern manner she said, "That's not a Christian name! Do you have a middle name?"

"Why yes, I do Sister. It's Mary."

With that reply she clasped her hands together and smiled, quite pleased with the answer.

"It doesn't get any better than that does it sister."

She went about her business and I left to go about mine. That brief encounter gave me pause to think about my name. Fifty years ago Dawn was an unusual name. I always hated it because everyone seemed to get it wrong. I was called Don or Donna, everything but Dawn. So, what's in a name? I certainly had not reflected on my own but on my ride home I found myself wondering why my mother chose the name Dawn. I began thinking about what it meant. It is the morning light, not a bright light, more of a gray light. I had lived a good deal of my life in a "gray area" but that had changed with the birth of a little girl named Katelin and the intercession of another child who laid in a coma in Worcester, Massachusetts. Both would make a profound difference in my life and set me forth on a journey of faith. This story is about the events that led to the change and the journey, which continues. My family received a miracle through faith, through prayer and through Jesus Christ. That single event has given meaning to my life and perhaps to my name. Dawn is the morning light, the soft light that announces the coming of the bright light of day—Jesus is the light. It brings me great joy to declare and make known the works of the Lord. May this story bring the 'light' of Christ into the lives of all who read it.

- *Dawn Curazzato*

Chapter One

Mike Wachowicz

$\mathcal{E}$very day when the alarm clock rings and announces the beginning of a new day, each of us arises and we begin our daily routine. We dance around the real issues of life by setting forth on our dreams and goals. Life is what happens between our routine and our plans for the future. Often we miss many splendid gifts because we are so caught up in achieving our goals. We take for granted that we are able to swing our legs over the side of the bed, walk down the hall, and take a warm shower. Our taste buds are awakened by a hearty breakfast, and our ears feast on the birds in song as the warmth of the sun rests on our backs. I too, took those things for granted, too busy to see the beauty in the simplicity of life all around me.

May 28th, 1989, started out like many spring days. It was a balmy sunny day, perfect for a ride in our new red convertible. It was just four days past my son's 14th birthday, and I decided to take him and two of his friends for ice cream. We stopped at our favorite place on Transit road. As we sat enjoying our ice cream, the sound of sirens rang out. Many police cars and an ambulance went flashing by. My son said, "Wow! There must be a big accident. Can we go see, Mom?"

My heart sinks whenever I hear a siren so of course I said "No". We finished our ice cream and took a slow ride home enjoying the sights and sounds of late spring.

The beauty of that day was shattered by a phone call we received as we entered our home. My son's friend, Mike Wachowicz was struck and killed by a car a short distance from where we had our ice cream. The screams of the siren were for him!

There is no greater loss than that of a child. It is the supreme sacrifice and one for which there are no consoling words. This event would have a profound effect on our lives. I was about to begin my "Journey of Faith".

Our first encounter with Mike Wachowicz happened about four years prior to the accident. We were sitting behind Mike and his family at St. Gregory the Great Parish during Mass. It is a large parish of about 5000 families. One could conceivably see a parishioner one week and perhaps never run into him again. I noticed my son staring at Mike during Mass. When Mike knelt, his head was below the top of the pew. Mike was a dwarf.

After Mass, misunderstanding his staring, I took my son, Joe, aside and said, "Don't ever make fun of someone less fortunate than yourself."

Joe proceeded to make a face, which I could not quite interpret, but before I could speak, he said, "Mom, that's Mike Wachowicz, do you know how popular that kid is?"

I was delighted to hear that, and I understood the look on my son's face to be one of bewilderment, because he did not view Mike as being handicapped. Perhaps the world had changed and some of the cruelties I had experienced as a child had diminished.

Mike went to school at St. Gregory's and Joe went to Maple West. Through a twist of fate they would soon become friends.

Joe displayed great athletic ability at a very young age. He was good in every sport he played, but he especially excelled in hockey. Hockey is a very big sport in the Western New York area, and Joe was making a name for himself. He was gregarious, and well liked in school and showed leadership qualities. After a parent-teacher conference, Joe's teacher, Mr. Crane, gave him a good report but closed with saying, "I feel a bit sorry for Joe. Success has come too soon for him and that can be difficult later on." The remark upset me, but I shrugged it off. It's not the worst thing to be said about a child. I did not know how prophetic that would prove to be.

Joe was about to enter Heim Middle school. Mike Wachowicz also chose to go there and before long he and Joe became fast friends. They were both popular with their classmates. Mike could win you over immediately with a smile that would light up a room. He was also generous, kind, and specialized in cheering up those who were down. Joe was a "jock" with a mischievous sense of humor, a determination to win, and a sensitivity he hid from all but his closest friends. Mike saw through Joe's toughness and the two of them teased each other good-naturedly. They shared lunch and gym class together. Many times Joe would carry Mike on his shoulders, get him his lunch, and anything else he needed. In gym class Joe always picked Mike first to be on his team.

When the travel hockey team Joe was on played for the State Championship, Mike cheered him on. When Joe injured his ankle and it looked like he might miss the rest of the Championship, Mike encouraged him. He cut out all of Joe's articles that were in the newspaper, and when Joe's team won the championship, with Joe being the leading scorer, Mike was one of the first to congratulate him. He always told Joe he was proud of him and knew that someday Joe would be playing in the NHL. Mike was never jealous for what he could not do, instead he was sincerely happy for those who were successful.

Class Night, an eighth grade graduation dance, was fast approaching and Joe asked his girlfriend, Stephanie to go. He also got a group of class-mates together to join them and they planned to get a limousine. Mike and Joe decided to rent the same tuxedo and the boys planned a few pranks. Joe was the class president therefore the pranks would be held to a mini-mum. It was to be a grand night filled with fun. There would be a dance and dinner. It was to be a time of friendship and laughter, a time of inno-cence, and a future filled with promise.

Mike Wachowicz was buried in his tux and the innocence and sweet-ness of childhood was buried with him. Those who knew him and loved him grieved for the irreplaceable loss and searched for an answer to the unanswerable, "Why"? They were left with precious memories and a hard lesson in the uncertainty of life.

There was a special assembly held at the school to honor Mike and plant a tree in his memory. Devastated by the loss of his friend, my son honored him in the only way he knew how, through a sports story. What follows is that story written by my son when he was 14 years old.

"Mike Wachowicz was my very good friend, and we had many great times together. I'd like to share a story that touched my heart. The last two years Mike and I shared lunch and Gym class. We had a lot of social time together. Mike started calling me "Dad". We used to look alike, walk alike, everything had to be alike. It was October, football season. In gym, I always picked Mike first to be on my team no matter who else was in class or how good they were. My team was seven and zero and we were playing for an undefeated season record and Mr. Hartman's popsicles. It was a good, hard fought game. The score was 28-28 with five minutes left. It was third down and we needed a touchdown to win. I called the guys into the huddle to call the next play. I had not thrown to Mike at all. Suddenly I felt a little tug on my arm. It was Mike, he said, "Joe, throw me the ball, I'm always open. They never cover me. I'll catch it, I promise!" I said "Okay Mike," with no intention of throwing him the ball. You see, winning was everything; it's all that mattered. The next play I threw the ball to a player in the end zone and he dropped it. It was the fourth down and we needed a touchdown. I looked over at Mike and saw the saddest eyes looking back at me. That down I faded back and looked for Mike. He was all alone hollering "Joe, throw me the ball!" I threw it and as it floated through the air I watched it go into the end zone and "Boom" Mike caught it! I had thrown the ball so hard it knocked him down. He got up, ran back to me, and jumped into my arms. He grabbed my face with his little hands and said, "We did it! I told you I'd catch it!" I said, "No, Mike, you did it, you're the hero!" I'll never forget the smile on his face. He may have been small in stature but he was a giant among us. He gave unselfishly from the depths of his heart. He was a hero. Mike, I miss you very much, and I hope I see you again someday. Thank you. Your friend, Joe.

My son had many athletic achievements, and many trophies, but I was never more proud of him as I was at the assembly for Mike Wachowicz. When he threw the football to Mike and it was "floating" through the air, so was his adolescence and when Mike caught the ball, my son became a man. In that split-second he learned winning isn't everything if it means losing a friend. Joe, I love you and I'm very proud of you. God bless you Mike for the valuable lessons you have taught us.

Chapter Two

Medjugorje

Chris Wachowicz is a beautiful woman outwardly and inwardly. She took the tragedy of her son's death and turned it into a ministry to help others. She is head of the Bereavement Ministry of Saint Gregory's and has helped countless people through the grieving process. Chris also conducts a Bible study which I had the good fortune to be a part of.

One day after church, Chris approached me and asked if I had heard of Medjugorje. I told her I had not and she went on to tell me it was a place like Fatima. The Blessed Mother was reportedly appearing to six children since 1981. I became very interested and Chris suggested I read a book called <u>Medjugorje: The Message</u> by Wayne Weible.

After reading the book, I decided someday I would go there. Shortly after my meeting with Chris, I learned Monsignor McNamara was allowing a presentation on Medjugorje to take place in Saint Gregory's. There was to be a film of the visionaries, a priest from that area, and a witness from several parishioners who had gone there. I was so excited I could hardly wait. When the day arrived I was very impressed with what I observed. I wanted more than ever to go there. I was struck by the look of peace on the faces of the parishioners who had visited Medjugorje. I immediately recognized this as something that was missing from my own life. When the presentation was over I walked up to the altar and said,

"Lord, that's what's missing in my life. Please let me know that peace!"

I asked for it and then I did what a lot of people do. I went back to my busy life and got comfortable with my routine.

Chapter Three

Lisa

My daughter Lisa was a typical teenager testing the waters of adulthood by breaking curfew and house rules. She was a good girl, though a little flaky during this period as she felt it her duty to challenge all authority. As a child she was shy, sweet, and always trying to please others. She never gave us a minute's worry and was an exceptionally good little girl. Once she turned 13, I found myself asking, "Who is this kid? Will I survive the teenage years?"

Approximately three years after the presentation on Medjugorje, I received a phone call that is every parent's worst nightmare. The caller said there had been an accident and we needed to get to the hospital. It was 4 AM on the Fourth of July. I ran to the front window looked out, and saw Lisa's car was not there. The hospital is only five minutes away, but it was one of the longest rides I ever took. I was filled with worry, anger, and fear. I wondered if she was dead or alive. When we reached the hospital the police told us Lisa's car had hit another car head-on and Lisa went partially through the windshield. She did not have her seat belt on, there was alcohol involved, and Lisa was not the driver. I was confused. We always told her not to let any one drive her car. She was also under the legal drinking age so we wondered where she had gotten the alcohol. We entered the emergency room filled with emotion and many unanswered questions. The nurse took us to a cubicle and pulled back the curtain. There laid my daughter with a nurse removing glass from her head. Her face had been miraculously spared. She was alive and I thanked God for that. Then I saw her leg. It was broken in half and the bone was sticking out of her shin. I felt about to faint when the doctor came in and said

Lisa had to be transferred to Erie County Medical Center (ECMC), a hospital better equipped to handle her injury. He said she would be all right and that sounded so good I did not ask what "all right" meant.

As the day progressed the pieces to the puzzle that led up to the crash began to fall into place. Apparently the girls used fake ID to get into a bar. Lisa's blood alcohol level was 0, but her friend who had been driving, had the equivalent of five drinks. I could not understand why Lisa had let her friend drive her car. We found out later that there were other girls involved and as Lisa was dropping them off at their houses she became sick and let her friend drive. Apparently when they were at the bar they split up, and Lisa was unaware of how much her friend had to drink. She was within a mile of our house when the accident occurred.

I had invited a group of friends and family for the Fourth of July holiday. After learning the details of the accident I could not help but feel a seesaw of emotions during the cookout. On one hand I was thanking God that she was alive and on the other hand I was ready to ring her neck. How many times had we told her "do not drink alcohol, do not drive with someone who has been drinking alcohol, ALWAYS wear your seat belt, drive carefully, obey the rules, and never let anyone else drive your car." I'm sure every parent gives similar advice to his or her children. Why must it always fall on deaf ears?

At ECMC, Lisa went into surgery and her leg and ankle were repaired as well as possible. Her ankle was crushed, and bone fragments were removed. Hardware was used to replace what was missing. She also had a long metal rod placed in her leg. Though she was badly bruised and had superficial cuts, she had no serious internal injuries. Lisa was in a cast for the remainder of the summer and had to go through a lot of physical therapy. The metal rod in her leg was removed a year later but the rest of the "hardware" remains. She has permanent disabilities, and arthritis, but she can live a normal life and we thank God for that. Lisa I love you, but I've noticed a lot of gray hair since that day!

Chapter Four

Joe

$\mathcal{I}$ had begun to go to daily Mass as often as possible. When I worked at Erie County Community College, I especially enjoyed the Mass celebrated by a very nice young priest, Father David Lee. It was a very small group and we would sometimes join hands around the Lord's Table. There was a sense of closeness, a sense of Holiness, and I liked beginning my day like that.

My interest in Medjugorje was still there but it was pushed to the background. I would read articles and books about it and these things would peak my interest and my desire to travel there. Then something would always happen to drag me back into my routine. We are creatures of habit and habits are hard to break. The day I walked up to the altar in church and asked God to know the peace of Medjugorje seemed so far away. I longed for that peace but seemed unable or unwilling to change the pattern of my life. The "seed" was planted and had begun to germinate but my awareness of it was dulled by my lifestyle.

It had been about three years since the death of Mike Wachowicz and Joe had continued to do exceptionally well in hockey. He had a very busy schedule, but remained focused on his schoolwork as well as his athletic commitments. He dreamed of one day playing in the NHL. Joe certainly exhibited a high skill level. He was a beautiful skater and very strong on his feet. Speed is not something you can teach, it is a God-given ability and Joe used it to his fullest advantage. It didn't hurt that he appeared to be a natural goal scorer. He almost always led his team in goals and points. He was very often the captain of his team.

I was far from enamored with the sport. They were unhappy years for me. Where I loved watching my son skate, I didn't like what travel hockey brought out in people. There are a lot of expenses involved and equal playtime does not figure into it. The coaches make that very clear, but parents tend to hear what they want to hear.

Joe had a lot of ice time; others did not, which made some parents angry. I heard some of the cruelest remarks I have ever heard in my life come from parents during these games. It makes you wonder who children's sports are for. Some of these people are obviously living their unfulfilled dreams through their children. Sometimes the remarks were so vicious they made me physically ill. I once had two mothers with boys on the same team as my son, tell me they prayed for my son to get hurt so somebody else had a chance!

I became very vocal in my opinions of some of the people in the league and that did not make me very popular. If someone behaved like a horse's ass then I was only too happy to let him or her know what I thought of them. If they were rude, crude or displayed unsportsmanlike conduct I was right in their face. Sometimes there were more fights in the stands than on the ice and I saw many parents get tossed from games.

My main source of unhappiness was the long season. It took me away from family and friends and forced me to be with people I otherwise would never have been with. Many times I did not go on tournaments because we could not afford the expense of bringing the whole family. Although that provided me time with Lisa and my friends, I was without my husband and son. If a wedding or some other occasion occurred which called for husband and wife, I either went alone or not at all. They were tumultuous, lonely years which would have ended much earlier had Joe not been a contender. There was always the buzz of earning a scholarship and perhaps the NHL. Since we are not a family of means that was a mighty big buzz! My son worked extra hard in trying to make his dream come true. My happiness was no sacrifice to see him realize his dream.

When Joe entered Nichols Prep School, which had its own hockey rink, and a very difficult academic curriculum, he rose to the occasion. Though he found the first year difficult he made the proper adjustments. He also experienced the setback of his first surgery. He was suffering from terrible pain that seemed to occur during rest periods and not during any athletic endeavors. He hid the pain from us until one day we were called to pick him up from school because he was ill. On the way home he told me to take him to the hospital. When I looked over at him, he was perspiring heavily and suddenly started kicking at the windshield of our vehicle because the pain was so intense. By the time I was done with the paperwork at the hospital, a doctor approached me, and told me Joe was resting comfortably. He told me Joe needed to see an urologist because he had Testicular Torsion. The pain is like a heart attack because the blood vessels in that area are strangulated. We took Joe to Dr. Greco who performed the surgery and he assured us that all went well and my son would be fine. As Joe was coming out of recovery he said, "Mom, I'm never going to be the same again!"

My heart sank to hear him talk like that but I assured him he would be better than ever. Joe's remarks disturbed me so I decided to speak to the doctor again. I asked him how Joe's condition occurred. I was told it was a congenital defect and where there is one there are usually others. I asked if we should run more tests, but he said no. He told us it was best to let Joe resume normal activities including his active sports life and not to look for trouble where there might not be any. After that I always had a wavering fear there was a time bomb ticking inside of my son. After the swelling went down Joe did return to all his activities and continued to perform at a high level. The parents of the boys on the team at Nichols were nice people, which made things very pleasant. It was during this period that I developed a friendship with Wendy Sittler, wife of Hockey Hall of Fame, Darryl Sittler. Wendy was a pretty girl with blond hair and laughing eyes. In fact, laughing was her specialty! She was a prankster and one always had to be on guard when she was around. I always had fun with her. She, Linda Fox (another hockey mom) and I were like the three musketeers, and it was basically a happy time. Years later all three of us would be facing other trials. It was Wendy's husband Darryl who told us Joe had all the necessary tools to play in the NHL, providing his level of play remained on par and barring any injuries.

Everything appeared to be going well until midway through his junior year. It was apparent something was wrong. Joe was maintaining his stats, but he would do his job, and take himself off the ice. This was very unlike him. He was suffering from severe muscle spasms, and one day after a particularly physical game his friend came out of the locker room and told us Joe was urinating blood. After questioning Joe, he admitted it had been going on for a while. We took him for tests and he experienced a life-threatening reaction to the dye injected into him to view his kidneys. It was a horrible experience in which Joe was given several shots to bring him around. The test results showed he had horseshoe shaped kidneys and the doctor could not be sure if both were working properly. This also was a congenital abnormality.

Joe had received many letters of intent from different colleges interested in him and he begged us not to disclose his recent results. He promised to be up front with us if he experienced any more physical problems. It was a promise he did not keep. Though he had good grades, his SAT scores were not very good. Rumors circulated about his health and his SAT scores and many of the schools who had shown interest pulled back. Even his coach labeled him as damaged goods. It was a particularly difficult time because Joe had worked so hard to reach his goals. The SAT scores proved he was a hard worker in school to attain the grades that he held. He ended up going to St. Lawrence College in upstate New York. The rules had changed just that year and he was given a conditional scholarship upon him keeping a certain grade point as well as making the hockey team. Joe received good grades and he liked the hockey coach very much. The coach felt he would fit well in the Division I program. During a tryout Joe got hit from behind and was injured. He underwent more tests. After ten years of abuse his young body was betraying him. These latest tests showed several discs were injured in his back, his vertebrae were misshapen, and his shoulders were shot. He needed more surgery and we brought him home. We began seeking the opinions of several doctors and decided to go with Dr. Moreland. He was a young doctor with a good reputation and a high rate of success. Before Joe went into surgery he reminded me of a poem he chose to write about in his senior year of high school. It was called "To an Athlete Dying Young" by A. E. Housman. He said, "That's me mom, it's about me."

It broke my heart to know he felt that way. When Dr. Moreland came out of surgery he informed us Joe had the discs of a 70-year-old man. He had removed 40 percent of the L4 and L5 discs, but nothing could be done for his ligaments. They were thin, like rubber bands which had lost their elasticity. The operation was not a success and Joe's dreams died in a heartbeat.

We let him go back to St. Lawrence and he threw himself into his studies. It was hard being in an area that was all hockey and where the bulk of his friends were hockey players. Still he did very well in school. His back problems persisted and when the school year was over he came home and entered spinal rehab. Because the accident occurred during tryouts and Joe had not officially made the team, the scholarship money was withdrawn. We could not afford to keep him in the school he had grown to love and once again he was disappointed. If the same set of circumstances had happened the year before he would have gotten to keep the scholarship. Joe sunk into a deep depression and remained in spinal rehab for a year. Knowing he had a condition that was not fixable was unbearable. I prayed a lot, I had to because now both of my children had permanent disabilities. I prayed to take their suffering if they could be spared. I turned to God for help. I pleaded, I cried and I hoped. I prayed to Mike Wachowicz to now carry his friend Joe on his angelic shoulders. I believe with all my heart he does.

Chapter Five

Shane

I had been reading some of the messages from the Blessed Mother in Medjugorje and she was calling for daily rosary. Though I prayed at night and went to Mass, I had not said the rosary in many years. I had to look up how to say it. It occurred to me how much the Blessed Mother suffered during the passion at Calvary. She too was a mother, she would understand how I felt. I would go to her and pray for her intercession for a healing for my children. I would go to her through the Rosary and bring my petitions to her in Medjugorje! At last, a plan of action, and one I was sure would help me find an answer to my prayers.

I thought the car accident would be a life changer for my daughter, as often happens. It was not. Lisa continued to do things her own way. We were often at odds and we drifted apart as I threw myself into my son's health concerns. Lisa was hurting too, and she felt left out during the recent tragedy that befell her brother. I worried about her and the strains of the last few years on the welfare of our family. I continued to pray, and I tried to be strong, but I fell short many times. My husband, Sam, was our "rock" during this period. He was dealing with so many struggles and handled them all with dignity and calm. He was father, friend, and mediator, never letting his brave exterior give way to the emotions that were surely churning inside of him. We were all looking for balance in our lives. We were all looking for a way to overcome these unexpected and unwelcome detours. Nothing changes one's path in life quicker than health issues. The peace I longed for, the peace I asked for seemed so distant. Perhaps it would never come to me, a chilling thought.

After experiencing an "empty nest" for a year, Joe moved home and enrolled in the University of Buffalo. He continued at spinal rehab and also took pain management courses. I was glad he was home so we could keep close watch on him.

Lisa tried college twice, once on our money and once on her own money. She never applied herself at being a serious student; instead she specialized in socializing. College is not for everyone, and a future in happiness is not promised to those who hold a degree. Every parent's wish for their child is to be happy, what path they take should not matter as long as they reach that goal. Lisa decided to invest in a duplex with the money she received as a settlement for her car accident. She was working a full-time job and I was helping her get settled in her home. I felt us growing closer again. Life is very much a quilt, each patch representing a certain phase. Each of my children had embarked on a new path brought about by an accident. We were all growing accustomed to this new routine when Lisa stopped by one day and announced she was pregnant! The baby's father was in college and there was no immediate plan to get married. My daughter came to me with this news expecting me to go off the deep end. I did not. Although I was hurt and certainly not happy about the situation, I was glad she chose life.

On Nov. 25th, 1995, my first grandchild, Shane Andrew McQuaid was born. He was born six weeks premature. His lungs were not fully matured and he was in respiratory distress. Shane was quickly transported to the Neonatal Intensive Care Unit (NICU) at Children's Hospital of Buffalo and placed on a ventilator to help him breathe. After five days he was ready to come home. I fell in love with him from the moment I saw him and I relished being his "Grammie". Lisa was in the hospital recovering from pre-eclampsia which brought about Shane's early arrival. Shane's dad and all my daughter's friends kept vigil at the hospital. Her room was filled with teddy bears, balloons, and flowers. I was happy my daughter had such good friends and a strong support system.

In just five short months Lisa found herself pregnant again. This time I did go ballistic! I let all the disappointment, the pain, and the fear I had inside of me spew out like a volcanic eruption. Of course that did not change the present situation, which had to be faced. I needed to be emptied of all emotion and I needed to know how to keep my family together. I did not know if Lisa was trying to destroy my hopes of a relationship with her or if this was a desperate cry for help. In the months previous to this she had landed an excellent job, had rented out the other half of her duplex and seemed more responsible. I babysat for her and my husband

and I helped out as best we could. I didn't know how she could handle everything with another baby on the way.

The father of the children, Patrick McQuaid, proposed in January 1995. They were married on September 1st of that same year. It is not the way most mothers envision their only daughter's wedding, but Pat and Lisa started dating when they were fourteen years old and shared a profound love for each other and a sincere love of children. I hoped for the best, but with divorce rates so high and with several strikes against them already, I wondered if their marriage would survive. These and other worrisome thoughts raced through my head as my husband walked our daughter down the aisle and placed her hand into the hand of the boy she had dated since middle school.

Chapter Six

Katelin

On February 11th, 1996, Katelin Amanda McQuaid was born. From the first time the doctor came into the room and told us there was a problem I knew our lives would be changed forever. The most sickening feeling rises from the pit of your stomach and fear becomes another entity encircling your life with crushing tentacles. Part of you wants to ask what's wrong, but the other part of you is afraid to hear the answer. It's a nightmare you tell yourself, and any minute you'll wake up and it will be all over. Reality checks in when you are led down a long corridor and told to wait outside the neonatal intensive care unit. Katelin was a full-term infant suffering from severe respiratory distress.

Lisa had her second cesarean section and was depressed because both of her babies had been taken from her immediately after delivery. She wanted to know what was wrong with her precious baby girl. We all wanted to know.

I went up to the resident in charge of Katelin and asked him what was wrong with her. He said he believed she had Wagner-Stickler's disease. He said it was like rheumatoid arthritis, most children diagnosed with the syndrome lose their eyesight by the time they reach 10 and sometimes there's mental retardation. The condition is painful and these children have flat facial features.

I had not seen Katelin yet, but Patrick had come out of the neonatal intensive care unit where the doctors put her on a ventilator to help her breathe. Katelin was in such distress during the delivery that her entire body quickly turned a deep, dark shade of purple. Pat brought me in to

16

see "our" little girl. As I approached her tiny bed there were tubes, machines, and monitors everywhere. Katelin had tubes going into her nose, and a tube going down her throat, which was taped, to her mouth. The tape prevented me from seeing her mouth or her chin. It was a most pitiful site. I thought I had already experienced heartbreak, but nothing prepared me for this. Shattering is the only word that comes close to describing that moment. I wanted to hold her and tell her we loved her. I wanted to tell her everything would be all right but there were too many tubes and instruments in the way. I just bent over her and whispered softly in her ear, "Grammie's here!"

If ever you lose your zest for life or get bored or unappreciative, I strongly suggest a visit to the NICU in Children's Hospital. I'll never forget the sights and sounds of the daily struggles of these tiniest souls. They fought valiantly to live. I will remember the cries of parents whose children did not live, and a man who slid down the wall onto the floor when the doctors told him his son had severe cerebral palsy. This is where you come to value how precious life is. You come to know the delicate balance lies more in God's hands than with the doctors. That is not to say that the doctors do not do everything humanly possible. They do and the nurses in the ICU are all angels of mercy. It is a difficult job with a high stress level. Special professionals are called to take these jobs. We were very lucky, all of the nurses who cared for Katelin were wonderful, as were most of the doctors.

Katelin was in the NICU for about two months in which her diagnosis changed several times. Not all tests are conclusive. Not all tests are accurate. That can be very frustrating when you're looking for answers. Sometimes there aren't any. We were told Katelin was deaf in one ear, and had a good percentage of hearing loss in the other ear. She would need a hearing aid. Her hands were always fisted with her thumb tucked inside. The doctor said this could mean a mental handicap. Tiny splints were made to help her keep her hands open. They identified a cataract in one eye, missing cartilage in her ear, and she held her arms stiff alongside her body. Some of the doctors had strong suspicions of severe cerebral palsy. Katelin also suffered from a motility disorder with severe reflux and was still unable to breathe on her own. Imagine not being able to breathe, or eat, two things we all take for granted. Doctors told us it could take up to a year to determine her mental capacity. She would need more surgery to control her reflux problem. No one could tell us what was in store for the future.

When the day came to release Katelin from the hospital I went up to the attending physician and asked what the final diagnosis was. I felt we were being sent home with more questions than answers. He said, "Look, you're lucky, you're getting to take your child home, some of these babies will never leave here!" I spun around and said, "Don't you dare compare her to the worst and tell us we are lucky. You compare her to the best and tell us what we can do to make her life better!"

He was frustrated and so was I. He just went about his business leaving me to my own recourse. A nurse who was standing nearby came over and said, "Don't worry about any of the things the doctors have told you. Take Katelin home and just love her! We have seen remarkable progress in children who are loved." I thanked her for her compassion and assured her that Katelin was loved and then I proceeded into the unknown.

Chapter Seven

Homecoming

There was much to be done for Katelin's homecoming. My daughter's dining room was turned into a hospital room with machines, monitors, and a lot of medical equipment. Katelin required round-the-clock nursing assistance except between the hours of 5 PM and 9 PM. Therapists came for early intervention and there was absolutely no privacy. All of us who would be helping in Katelin's care were taught how to change her trache and suction her. Lisa and Pat were also taught how to give her meds and her feeds and how to flush out her lines into her veins and her stomach. Katelin had motility problems and when all her surgeries were done she would eventually have the trache, a tube in her stomach, a tube in her intestines, and a tube directly into her heart to give her hyper alimentation. This was a most dangerous situation as an infection near the site can be fatal. Katelin was also susceptible to infection through her open airway. There were so many things to deal with it was overwhelming.

Lisa had to work full-time because Pat was still in college and he worked nights as a waiter. I babysat Shane, as the nurses cared for Katelin. We had a full schedule of work, babysitting, doctor appointments, and the average everyday necessities that needed to be tended to as well. A marriage that starts out with two children, one being handicapped, no privacy, and lots of financial problems certainly had the odds stacked against it. Yet, Lisa and Pat grew closer together. Patrick participated in every aspect of Katelin's care. He was absolutely wonderful, and he learned everything that was necessary for her medical care including emergency procedures. Lisa was a mother and a nurse combined. She was gentle, loving, and attentive. I was very proud of both of them. During

19

this time we were given these two pieces about having a handicapped child, "The Beauty of Holland" and "God's Special Child".

The Beauty Of Holland

I am often asked to describe the experience of raising a child with a disability—to try to help people who have not shared that unique experience to understand it, to imagine how it would feel. It's like this....
When you're going to have a baby, it's like planning a fabulous vacation trip—to Italy. You buy a bunch of guidebooks and make your wonderful vacation plans. The Coliseum. The Michelangelo David. The gondolas in Venice, You may learn some handy phrases in Italian, It's all very, very exciting.
After months of eager anticipation, the day finally arrives. You pack your bags and off you go. Several hours later, the plane lands. The flight attendant comes in and says, 'Welcome to Holland'.
"Holland?!?", you say. "What do you mean, Holland? I signed up for Italy! I'm supposed to be in Italy. All my life I've dreamed of going to Italy."
But there's been a change in the flight plan. They landed in Holland and there you must stay
The important thing is that they haven't taken you to a horrible, disgusting, filthy place, full of pestilence, famine, and disease. It's just a different place.
So you must go out and buy new guidebooks. And you must learn a whole new language. And you will meet a whole new group of people you would never have met.
It's just a different place. It's a slower-paced than Italy, less flashy than Italy. But after you've been there for a while and you catch your breath, you look around, and you begin to notice that Holland has windmills. Holland had tulips. Holland even has Rembrandts.
But everyone you know is busy coming and going from Italy, and they're all bragging about what a wonderful time they had there. And for the rest of your life, you will say, "Yes, that's where I was supposed to go. That's what I had planned."
And the pain of that will never, ever, ever go away, because the loss of that dream is a very significant loss.

But if you spend your life mourning the fact that you didn't get to Italy, you may never be free to enjoy the very special, the very lovely things about Holland.

Author unknown

Heaven's Special Child

A meeting was held quite far from earth
"It's time again for another birth,"
Said the angel of the Lord above
"This special child will need much love.
Her progress may seem very slow;
Accomplishments she may not show,
And she'll require much extra care
From all the folks she meets down there.
She may not laugh or run or play
Her thoughts may seem quite far away
In many ways she won't adapt.
And she'll be know as "handicapped'.
So lets be careful where she's sent
We want her life to be content.
Please Lord, Find the parents who
Will do this special job for you.
They may not realize right away
The leading role they're asked to play,
But with the child from above,
Comes stronger faith and richer love,
And soon they'll know the privilege given
In caring for this gift from heaven.
Their precious child so meek and mild
Is "Heaven's very special child"

Author Unknown

Chapter Eight

Faith

$\mathcal{I}$ had very little spare time but when I found some, I spent it at the library researching Katelin's condition. I would copy information and give it to Lisa to have questions ready for the doctors. At this point in time Katelin went from one crisis to another. It seemed we could not go two weeks without a hospital visit. She had had multiple surgeries and also had several serious infections. After one such episode I was at the library checking on some of Katelin's medications, and I looked up hyper alimentation through the Broviac line in her heart. There were many dangerous side effects, one being damage to the liver, and other major organs. I also came across the disturbing information that 75 percent of marriages in which a child dies or is handicapped fail. I sat there and cried and begged God to help us.

There were many close calls and worries to numerous to mention, but there is always one incident that stands out above the others. This particular incident would completely change the course of action.

One evening I went over to Lisa's to help out, and found Lisa and Patrick crying. After more tests the doctors told them there was a possibility the trache and feeding tube might remain throughout her life and her deafness was permanent. Lisa said, "If she can't hear, breathe, eat, and possibly may go blind by the time she's 10, how will she know we love her?" Patrick just sobbed and said, "My poor little girl".

That was the first time I saw Pat crying. He was always such a trooper. It broke my heart to see him so shaken up, and I could not find anything positive to say to help them out. I felt so helpless!

Lisa walked over to me and said words I never wanted to hear. She said, " Mom, my little girl is never going to the prom, she's never going to dance, or get married, or have children of her own!"

I stopped her from going on by hugging her and saying, " Lisa, don't you say that! We don't know if that's true. The doctors can't even give us a straight answer. They don't know what she has, or what caused her condition, so don't count her out!" At that, Lisa began crying very hard and said, " Look at her mom! Look at her! What kind of life is she going to have?"

I told Lisa I was not going to stick around and listen to talk like that and I walked out. I got into my car and drove away, but I had to pull off the road because I was crying so hard, I could not see. I was not crying because I didn't believe what Lisa had said, but because I did! The street I pulled over on was John James Parkway, in Amherst and it did not occur to me until years later that those are the names of two of the apostles. It was there in the car, at that moment, I made a deal with God. I made promises. Oh, I know people say you can't make a deal with God. Well I plead ignorant and Irish. I didn't know any better, and everything I said was straight from the heart, and that makes all the difference in the world!

The Irish are a long-suffering people whom God has blessed with an extra helping of Faith. We complain with the best of them, but we have also been given a delightful sense of humor, which helps us deal with the most difficult situations. I thank God for the Faith He has given me, and I capitalized the F in Faith because it should be. I asked for a miracle, and you do not get one without Faith! There are many examples of this in the Bible. In Mark, chapter 6 verses 25-34 we see the woman afflicted with a hemorrhage for 12 years and she say's, "

"If I just touch his clothes, I shall be cured". And what does Jesus say to her? " Daughter, your Faith has saved you. Go in peace and be cured of your affliction"

In Matthew, chapter 8 and verses 5 through 13, we see the healing of the Centurion's servant. When the Centurion asks for a cure he says to Jesus, " Lord I am not worthy to have you enter under my roof, only say the word and my servant will be healed." Jesus replied, "Amen, I say to you, in no one in Israel have I found such faith. You may go, as you have believed, let it be done for you."

These are just two examples but there are others that show Faith is a key ingredient to a miracle. I don't wish to share all my promises, but I will discuss one later. There is no special formula for a miracle, but it certainly helps to ask, seek, and knock with faith. The most perfect prayer is the one from the heart.

When I was done crying, complaining, promising, and praying, I found I had chosen a new direction. Since the doctors could not give us the answers we were looking for, then I would go to the Divine Healer. I would take Katelin to Medjugorje. The plan was set, and all I needed was a way to get this sick child on a plane with all her medical equipment and the money to do so. It was quite a challenge and most of the people I confided in thought it was a crazy idea because the hospitals in the former Yugoslavia were very poor. To get there, I would have to get a home equity loan. Katelin continued to have problems and was in the hospital often. I became discouraged, but did not give up on my plan. In the meantime a lady from church encouraged me to take Katelin to a healing Mass. I had never been to one before and I did not know what it entailed. When you're not exposed to life changing situations there's no need to explore new avenues. This would be one of many new paths Katelin would put me on. When the Lord puts us through the "fire" for our purification it is for our own good. He knows what is best for us and we must pray to know His will, and to do it!

Chapter Nine

Suffering

Suffering is part of our purification. It is the pupa stage of Christianity. Before we become a beautiful butterfly we must suffer. We only have two choices, to go toward Christ or away from him. That may be one of the most important choices we make. When we hear about a tragic accident, a drunk driver taking the life of an honor student, or the abuse of a child, we tend to get angry with God. We question where he is amidst all these injustices and why does he allow these things to happen. We do not suffer because of God, we suffer because of our sins! There is a great deal of sin in the world today.

It is also important to know there is power in suffering when it is united to Christ's suffering. Everyone 50 and older may remember complaining about a headache, or stomachache, and being told by your mother, or grandmother, to offer it up to God for the conversion of poor sinners. There is great saving power in offering up your suffering for someone else. This is the main Faith journey of victim souls.

There have been many victim souls throughout church history. Padre Pio, who suffered the stigmata (wounds of Christ), Bernadette of Lourdes, and the children of Fatima to name a few. It was little Jacinta of Fatima who said," If you knew the value of suffering, you would pray to suffer more!" She was six years old when she said that and I'm sure there are many people who feel this is a crazy statement. The fact is, these people are the chosen ones. They receive Divine knowledge and have Divine understanding. They usually are visited by an angel, the Blessed Mother, or Jesus, and are asked if they would be willing to suffer to save souls. They have free will, but choose to do God's will. Suffering to save those who are lost becomes their "soul" purpose in this life. Thank God we have these suffering servants. We may not understand the entire scope of it, but it is comforting to know these people are somewhat of a bridge between heaven and Earth. If we understand that concept of suffering we know why euthanasia is wrong. We do not have the right to end our life, even if we have a progressive terminal illness. God gives us life and he gives us crosses throughout our lives to bring us closer to him. He also gives us the grace to carry our crosses if we just ask him.

Perhaps in our journey home we will receive a "visit" and we may be asked to join our suffering to Christ's to save a soul. We may be saving a son, daughter, mother, father, or a friend. The soul we may be saving is our very own!

Two thousand years ago Jesus laid down his life for our salvation. It was the most unselfish act in human history. This act of unfathomable love should be commemorated in every church by displaying a crucifix in a visible spot. It's not a morbid thing to do. It is an honorable thing to do! His suffering brought us eternal life!

Chapter Ten

My Gethsemane

*A*s Christians we are called to be comforters. We're told to embrace the cross and console the suffering. Today people run from it as if it were contagious! When we hear a friend or loved one is ill, we send cards, flowers, or fruit baskets, and we think we have done our duty. We avoid a visit at all costs because we are too busy. Being too busy is the greatest cancer of our times, and it is the biggest cause of the sins of omission. It is epidemic! The greatest gift you can give someone who is suffering is the gift of your time. Pay a visit! There may be some awkward moments, but the person you spend time with will remember your visit long after the fruit has been eaten, the flowers have died, and the card is thrown away.

When Katelin was born some of my friends made some kind gestures, but very few visited! During the entire time she was in NICU at Children's Hospital I had friends, family, and people from work tell me, "Maybe it would be better if the Lord just took her."

I still get angry when I think how callous and cold that remark is. On one occasion when a certain person made that remark for the third time I snapped. I told her how cruel it was, how it tore my heart out every time I heard it. The response to me was, " I'm only thinking of you, you will have no life!" Perhaps these people meant well, but it's better to say nothing at all then to make an unkind comment.

My friend's husband died of a heart attack at 52 years old. I remember standing with her at his coffin when a woman came up to her and said, "Don't cry Joanie, you're young, you'll marry again." We were both stunned at the woman's "consoling words". We really need to think about

27

what we're saying to someone who is suffering. Our words should reflect compassion. Some comments, even when they are true, are inappropriate at these times.

During the time Katelin was so ill several girls I had grown up with asked me to meet them for lunch. I was thrilled, as I had not been out in a long time, and I had not seen them in a while. As we waited for lunch, one of my friends took out pictures of her grandson. She passed them around and we told her how adorable he was. I reached into my purse to bring out pictures of Katelin, and my friend held up her hand to stop me. She said, "I can't look at things like that, they make the sick."

I was stunned and it got very quiet for what seemed like an eternity. The waitress brought our lunch, and I really don't remember the rest of that afternoon. I honestly don't know how I made it through that lunch, but I saw very little of my friends after that. If you met these people you would like them. They are not bad people, perhaps a little inconsiderate, and maybe materialistic, but not bad. When a friendship has lasted many years you tend to overlook a lot. When you are suffering your friends become your lifeline and you wear them like a life jacket because that's what they are. Weaknesses and flaws are displaced by need. A friendship is truly tested during the trials of suffering. I lost almost every friend during this time.

I came home from the hospital one day and found myself sitting in the kitchen, alone in the dark. I felt surrounded by a feeling of impending doom when I suddenly cried out to the Lord, "Must I bear this too?" As soon as I said that, I realized this was my Gethsemane. Our Lord's friends disappointed him, and left him alone too. They ran from him during his time of need. Why should it be any different for me? As I pondered the question, I answered it myself, "Because Lord, I am but a weak woman, please take this cup from me!" I continued to plead and to complain instead of saying "Your will be done."

My world was changing once again. All that I knew, and was comfortable with was disappearing and I only had two choices, to move towards God, or away from him!

"Okay Lord, here I am, now how about that miracle we talked about!

Chapter Eleven

The Dominican and Carmelite Nuns

Though I still had every intention of taking Katelin to Medjugorje, I was having trouble putting the plan into action. As I tried to work out the details I began seeking the Lord in earnest. I also made sure Katelin was put on as many prayer chains and rosary offerings as possible. Through a woman at church, I was put in touch with the Dominican and Carmelite nuns. What a gift these prayerful women are! They have helped me through some of my darkest hours and I maintain a close tie to them. I love them all, but I have a special fondness for a Dominican nun known as, "Sister Mary Mystery", to me. She has inspired me, and has written many beautiful faith filled letters. I'm quite sure she is a gift from God to my family and me. I pray to meet her someday. Indeed, I have asked to do just that, but she is cloistered and her vows do not permit it.

If you ever experienced a dry spell in prayer or find yourself in the grips of fear turn to these wonderful nuns and let them pray for you. Many times I have experienced great comfort knowing these remarkable women were lifting me up in prayer. They are dedicated to a life of poverty, chastity, humility, silence, obedience, and prayer. They grow the food they eat, can vegetables and fruit, wash clothes, and do all sorts of manual labor. One day while visiting the Dominicans, one of the volunteers told me all the nuns were fasting on creamed corn. I was shocked, but told not to worry, the nuns will pray, and God will take care of them. I was fascinated by their complete trust in God to provide for them. Sometimes this comes through lay people bringing food to the nuns or giving a donation.

While visiting the Carmelite monastery the nuns began to sing the Divine Office. If you ever want to hear the angels sing visit 75 Carmel Road at 2:00 PM. Their serene voices fill the chapel and when the singing stops they pray the rosary. It is quite moving and sure to bring a tear to your eye. The monastery is beautiful and I especially like praying before a statue of the "Bridegroom" on the left-hand side of the chapel, as you come in. It is a statue of Our Lord with a crown of thorns and holding a reed, which is extremely lifelike. There are also several statues of St Therese, the little Flower, whom I have great devotion to and whom I call on daily. It is a wonderful place to visit and I have a found great peace there.

The Dominican chapel is also lovely, and they have perpetual adoration, which is so dear to my heart. I love my visits there as well. When you write prayer requests they send a nice personalized note with a prayer card or a particular devotional. How I love my letters from "Sister Mary Mystery", and what an example of Faith all these women are. We are so lucky to have them. Please pray for them, and for stronger, sincere callings to the religious life. If you would like to make a donation please send them to, the Carmelite Nuns, at 75 Carmel Road, Buffalo, New York 14214 or the Dominican Nuns at 335 Doat Street, Buffalo, New York 14211

Chapter Twelve

The Healing Mass

$\mathscr{I}$ found out there was to be a healing Mass at St. Gregory's and I wanted Katelin to be blessed. I called the rectory and spoke with one of our priests and appraised him of Katelin's condition. I asked him a few questions concerning the Mass, as I had never been to a healing service before. I told him Katelin had a trache and needed frequent suctioning by a machine that was quite loud. The priest told me to meet him at the back of the church where he would give Katelin a blessing, and the anointing of the sick. After speaking to him I called Lisa and my parents to tell them the arrangements. I told them how wonderful this priest was, and how I was looking forward to them meeting him.

The day before the healing Mass I went to confession and the priest I had spoken to on the phone happened to be the confessor. A little bit of time had passed since we had spoken and I wanted to make sure I understood his instructions. So I told him I was a little apprehensive about bringing Katelin, as it was dangerous for her to be around a lot of people, because of her open-air way, and she could not be out for too long. He assured me he understood and again said he would meet us at the back of the church.

When we got to church Lisa's in-laws, Richard and Kathy McQuaid and my parents met us. The McQuaids are very kind people with a strong devotion to their family. We are blessed to now be a part of their family, and my daughter's lucky to have such nice in-laws.

Ginny Lauria and Gerry Mergenhagen, members of the Ladies of Charity, greeted us and helped us get settled. I told them about my conversation with the priest and Ginny let him know we were waiting for him. Mass began, and he did not come. We waited thinking he would come back at any moment, but as the blessings began he stayed upfront. Several other priests were concelebrating the Mass as well and finally Father Paul of the Consolatas came back and blessed Katelin. He was very gentle and most kind. When my priest from St. Gregory's came back to us he said, "Did someone get to you?" I replied Yes, Father, but should we wait for the anointing with oil?" And he said, "Yes, I'll be right back". With that he walked away and never came back! My mother leaned over and whispered, "Either he is deliberately trying to hurt you, or he has the shortest memory in history! This is the priest you think is so wonderful? Well I don't think much of him at all."

I did not know what to think. I had spoken to him the night before and he was well aware of how sick Katelin was. He could not have forgotten. She was an innocent little baby. What could possibly have made him so abrupt and uncaring? I had always spoke highly of him and found his Masses to be very inspirational I was deeply hurt and after that day, I always questioned his sincerity. His actions were very confusing to me. Though I felt slighted, I had far more pressing matters to concentrate on.

During my daughter's pregnancy doctors found a tumor on her thyroid. They were unable to do anything about it until after Lisa had the baby. Lisa never said anything to us about it. When Katelin was born so sick, Lisa let herself go to take care of Katelin. The tumor had grown and was now entangled in her vocal cords. She had to have it out right away. Hospitals were becoming a way of life in our household. We were all worried that the tumor might be cancerous.

Before her surgery I went before the Blessed Sacrament and prayed, "Dear God, please let Lisa be all right. Shane and Katelin need their mother. I need her!"

Lisa was operated on at Sister's Hospital and had half her thyroid removed. There was no sign of cancer, thank God! The doctor said she may be left with a raspy voice, but compared to cancer that was certainly no big worry.

We all rallied to set up schedules to visit Lisa at the hospital, and also help Patrick with the children so he could go to school and work. I do not know what I would have done through all of this without the help of my mother. The lady is a saint! She has always been there for me throughout my life and she was the one constant strength through all of this. She was always the extra pair of helping hands, the one I could always depend on. With everyone working full-time jobs, many times the help came down to my mother and me. She was excellent with Shane and Katelin. All of her grandchildren love her in a very special way. This is a true testimony to the kind gentle woman she is.

Chapter Thirteen

Family Ties

$\mathcal{M}$y mother, Ginger Faley, grew up in the projects, the first born of four children to Frank and Edith Bittle. They struggled, especially during the Depression years, but my mother remembers her childhood as happy and loving. She was a beautiful young woman with auburn hair and green eyes. She had many suitors, but gave her heart to a blue-eyed, blond, Irishman, Milo P. Faley.

My father was a Father Baker's boy, raised by the priests for many years while my grandmother worked and frequented the pubs. We never knew my grandfather and details of his existence are sketchy. We know at one point my grandmother retrieved my father and after a short reunion he joined the Navy and fought in World War II. When the war was over he married my mother and started a family. I was their first-born, born on June 28th, 1950, a holy year, and also the feast day of St. Iraneus. We lived in the projects during the early years and eventually my parents bought a home in Kenmore, where I spent the remainder of my years growing up. There were five children, four girls, and a boy. My parents did their very best to provide a good and happy home for us. Kenmore had a good school system, and still does. It is the neighborhood of hard-working people, and was a great place to grow up.

Many times my father worked two jobs to make ends meet. Sometimes we did not see him until Sunday. There were also times he was out of work for lengthy periods. It was during one of those periods my brother Michael became very ill. He cried a lot, but when my mother took him to the doctor he could find nothing wrong. He told her to let him cry and my mother told him she felt his cries were cries of pain. The doctor thought my mother was overreacting and ignored her pleas.

One night, shortly thereafter, I heard loud voices and my brother was crying very hard. When I woke up the next day he was gone, and my grandma Bittle told me he had to go to the hospital. Michael had to have a kidney removed due to some abnormality, which was never discussed. People whispered about illnesses back then, they were not discussed, especially in front of children. My parents were very upset and stressed because of Michael's suffering and mounting medical bills. It was the first time I remember being afraid and not feeling secure.

Aside from that I remember my childhood being most happy. My mom would pop popcorn and tell stories and take us to see a Disney movie. I especially liked, Snow White, Cinderella, Bambi, and The Ugly Duckling. We always had the best Christmas, mom was very artistic, and our tree decorations were exquisite! Our house was transformed into a Christmas wonderland. She was a great cook, and made many special cookies, and goodies of the season.

One Christmas some ladies from church came over with a huge basket. It was filled with an assortment of food. We squealed with delight, but my mother cried, and dad did not look happy either. I did not understand until years later that we were poor. My parents saw to it that we had what we needed and provided us with the things money can't buy. We never felt different or underprivileged on the contrary we were happy.

When my father was out of work from the steel mills or Bell Aerospace he would often do a novena and make the first Fridays. He would always find work when he did that and I was exposed to that kind of faith while growing up. I went to Mass every Sunday and frequent confession, my father often told me stories about Padre Pio and Fatima.

I remember one particular story of a friend of my fathers who had the good fortune to go to San Giovanni Rotundo and have a confession with Padre Pio. When he returned from Italy he told everyone about this amazing priest who bore the wounds of Christ. He told my father when he finished confession; Padre Pio asked him if that was all he had to confess. My dad's friend told him that it was and Padre Pio proceeded to tell the man everything he had done since he was six years old! His visit with this remarkable priest changed his life.

My father has a very strong devotion to Padre Pio, and claims he has smelled the scent of sweet tobacco, which is sometimes associated with a visit from the dear Padre. My mother has teased my father about this, and suggested perhaps he had drunk one too many beers! Neither of my parents smokes. One evening my father began shouting for my mother to come quickly. When she ran to see what was wrong she found my father with a beautiful smile, and the room was filled with the scent of sweet tobacco! She swears she too experienced this phenomenon. It is well known that Padre Pio had the gift of bilocation and some say he had the gift to read souls. There are many books about the life of Padre Pio. I especially liked <u>Padre Pio, The Stigmatist</u> by Father Charles Carty.

The other story I was fascinated with was Fatima. There are many books on this subject, but I think one of the best is a more recent book called <u>The Fatima Prophecies</u>, by Thomas Petrisko. It is an in-depth, excellent, account of what happened in Fatima and what the prophecies mean to the future of the world. It also discusses many of the major Marian apparitions and their meaning.

As a child I had announced to my father if I had been alive during the apparitions I would have gone to Fatima. Surely there was nothing more wonderful then being close to the Blessed Mother and seeing the sun dance in the sky! Perhaps a little seed was planted then.

I now had a chance to visit a place just like Fatima where the Blessed Mother has reportedly been appearing to six children since 1981 in the former Yugoslavia. The Blessed Mother gives the visionaries' messages for the world and before her apparitions are over, each of the visionaries will have received 10 secrets. Her messages are simple, but profoundly spiritual and are centered on her son Jesus. She invites us to live His gospel. Millions of pilgrims have visited Medjugorje since 1981 and it is not uncommon to see people walking the streets with their rosaries in hand. It is also not uncommon for pilgrims and the locals to spend three hours a day in Saint James church. The Mass is the main focal point of the day. The Blessed Virgin made an exciting promise, she said she would leave a visible and permanent sign on Mount Podbrdo where she first appeared in Medjugorje. This sign would be proof to the world that it was indeed the Blessed Mother who was appearing in Medjugorje.

I prayed to find a way to get my sick grandchild to Medjugorje where I would ask the Blessed Mother to intercede for a healing from her merciful son, Jesus. I had every confidence this would happen.

Lisa recovered fairly quickly from her surgery, but Katelin continued to struggle. She was not gaining any weight and was not thriving. When I picked her up she felt stiff, almost like rigor mortis was setting in. She would foam at the mouth, too weak to swallow her saliva. I feared she was dying, and grew very impatient. I needed to do something and I needed to do it fast. With all our problems, a trip to Medjugorje seemed to be an impossibility.

Chapter Fourteen

Audrey Santo

To Risk

To laugh is to risk appearing the fool
To weep is to risk appearing sentimental
To reach out for another is to risk involvement
To expose feelings is to risk exposing yourself
To place ideas and dreams before the crowd is to risk loss
To love is to risk rejection
To live is to risk dying
To hope is to is to risk despair
To try at all is to risk failure
But risk we must,
Because the greatest hazard of all is to risk nothing
For those who risk nothing, do nothing, have nothing are nothing!

On Good Friday of 1997 my dad called and asked if I could come over right away. He sounded very excited and he told me he had something I must see. When I arrived at my parents home my dad told me to sit down, and proceeded to play a video from Eternal Word Television Network (EWTN), which he had seen on Mother Angelica. It was the story of little Audrey Santo. She was a three-year-old child who fell into the family swimming pool and had a near drowning accident. She was revived but was given too much Phenobarbital and lapsed into a coma. She remains in a state called Akinetic Mutism. Her mother, Linda took her to Medjugorje to pray for healing. Instead, Audrey went into cardiac arrest, and ended up in Mostar hospital. She coded four times. Because her condition was so critical she was not allowed to go home by commercial airliner. Linda had to contact a United States senator who got a military medical plane to fly from Germany to Yugoslavia to transport her home at the cost of $25,000! This was added to the cost of the trip, which was $8000. Linda had to secure a home equity loan and bring her daughter home in virtually the same state she left in. After this terrible incident Linda did not lose her faith, on the contrary her faith grew! Although this may sound unusual it would pale in comparison to the events, which would soon begin occurring in the Santo home after the trip to Medjugorje. Heaven was about to pay a visit to the Santo home.

In his book In God's Hands, by Thomas Petrisko, it is revealed that Audrey was allowed in the room where the Blessed Mother appears to the visionaries. It is related that the Blessed Mother appeared to Audrey and asked her if she wished to be healed or if she would be willing to suffer to save souls. She was four years old at the time, and was given divine understanding. She chose to be a victim soul: a suffering servant. These are God's chosen ones, who have the option of exercising free will, but choose to do our Lord's will. After her trip to Medjugorje it is reported Audrey received the wounds of Christ on Good Friday and various holy days. There are also reports of healings, weeping statues, and bleeding communion wafers.

I zeroed in on the healings and tended to block out the rest. Once I saw Audrey with the trache and feeding tube just like Katelin had I knew this was the place we had to go. Where Medjugorje seemed impossible for us, Worcester MA, was a definite possibility. This would be my Medjugorje, and it did not escape me that Audrey had a Medjugorje connection.

On Easter Sunday my daughter Lisa saw the video and said, "Oh, Mom, can we go there? I answered her "Of course we can!" A simple exchange of words and our journey seeking the Divine Healer began. We would find him at the bedside of a girl who lay in coma in Worcester MA.

The only information we had was the name of the church from the EWTN tape. Lisa called the church from work while I called the airlines from home to book a flight. Because we had not booked a flight in advance I was quoted a price of $1066 for the three of us. I did not have the money and put it on my charge card.

When Lisa reached a priest at Christ the King parish she was told we needed an appointment to visit Audrey, and he gave her a number to call. Lisa called the phone number she was given, and a woman answered. She told Lisa since the story was shown on EWTN there was now a waiting list of up to one year. At that news Lisa began crying she told the lady that

Katelin had been in the ICU for two months, and had a trache and feeding tube just like Audrey. Lisa then told her about the recent operation to remove half of her thyroid. There was great urgency to the words Lisa spoke. Finally the woman asked if we could be there on Wednesday, she would squeeze us in. "Yes!" was the resounding answer, and when Lisa told me the lady's name was Mary it brought a smile to my face. Tuesday, April 1st, 1997 would be our travel day. Then we would be at Audrey's Wednesday April 2nd. All the arrangements were made rather quickly, and I was amazed at how smoothly it transpired.

Chapter Fifteen

The Trip

The night before we left Katelin's nurse helped Lisa pack all of Katelin's equipment and medications. The next morning we woke up to the news that a Nor'easter storm had hit and crippled the East Coast. All flights were canceled. We would not be able to get a flight into Worcester. Lisa called me and was extremely upset. She said, "Now what are we going to do mom?" To which I replied, "I'll drive there!"

It is not a smart or a responsible action to drive into a blizzard and it is understandable that my husband did not support my decision. To make matters worse, my mother called to say she was sorry the trip was off. When I told her it was very much on, she said, "You can't be serious! Lisa just had surgery, Katelin has multiple problems, and you are responsible for their lives! How could you go ahead with this? If anything happens to them God help you!"

We hung up. I cried, and felt God's help was exactly what I needed. I called my church and asked to speak to a priest, any priest, and I was told they were all busy, but the Deacon was available. I told the secretary to please put him on the line. When he came to the phone I immediately fell apart and I told him what I was going to do and I asked him to pray for our safety. Deacon Jim, may God bless him, said something very profound. He said "You don't have to go all the way to Worcester in a blizzard to see this person, when God is right here". I told him I knew that intellectually, but I had a force in me directing me to go. I now realize it was the Holy Spirit, but I did not know that then.

Deacon Jim promised to pray for our safety and with that comforting thought we got into the car and drove into a blizzard. We listened intently to the radio. At every point where the thruway was closed as we reached it, it had been reopened! It seemed so strange that we did not see one snowflake! Katelin needed frequent suctioning and we took our time stopping often along the way. We drove into the blizzard armed only with faith, and for the first time we felt we had taken charge of the situation. We were filled with hope!

As we drove into Worcester the effects of the blizzard were everywhere. There was about three feet of snow and the roads were icy. When we reached our hotel and began unpacking Lisa shouted "Oh, No! As I turned I said, "What's wrong?" Lisa proceeded to tell me the nurse had not packed the pole for Katelin's gravity induced feeds and the proper tubing was also missing! The baby needed her Meds and feeds and this presented us with a dilemma. I had been driving for eight hours would I now have to turn around and drive home or could we rig something up ourselves? We took a light fixture off the hook in the ceiling that would work for the gravity induced feeds, but without the proper tubing it was useless. We pulled out the local phone book and began calling hospitals, we found one who felt they could help us. We alerted the front desk to our situation and a very nice young man and young girl offered to drive Lisa to the hospital. They assured us the hospital was only ten minutes away. After an hour and a half I became alarmed. Katelin needed her meds and feeds. I called the desk, but the shift had changed and no one knew who took Lisa or what hospital she was at. To make matters worse, I heard sirens and when I looked out the window of our hotel there was a terrible accident. I was convinced it was Lisa. The enormity of the risk I had taken came crashing in on me. I called my husband at home and began screaming into the phone that Lisa had been in an accident, the baby was in distress, and I was about to faint! Then I did what people do when they do not want to take responsibility for their own actions, I called my husband some colorful names, and blamed him for my situation. If he had driven, if he had supported me, if if…. When I finished my tirade I told him to get us help right away and proceeded to give him the wrong number! Five minutes later the phone rang. When I picked it up it was the young girl who had driven Lisa to the hospital along with her boyfriend. She said she was very sorry but they had to go to three different hospitals before they found one who could help. Lisa was being trained on a machine that would be able to help Katelin and they would be coming back to the hotel shortly. Now I felt like the Saturday Night Live character, Roseanne Roseannadanna, played by Gilda Radner. I had to call my husband back and say "Never mind!"

It was 2 AM by the time we got Katelin hooked up and fed. The machine made a loud buzzing noise throughout the night. It was impossible to sleep. I could not get over how quickly my faith had diminished when really put to the test! I thought of Linda Santo, and all she went through in Medjugorje. Her Faith held strong and true. Tomorrow I would meet this remarkable woman.

The following morning we drove back to the hospital to return the machine Katelin had used and from there we were given directions to Audrey's house. We were told the seriously ill could be dropped off at Audrey's home while the other pilgrims were to wait for a ride at Christ the King church. As we approached the house two nuns and a priest were also arriving, I felt confident letting Lisa and Katelin go with them. I left and waited for my ride at Christ the King church.

Lisa and Katelin were invited to go into Audrey's room with the priest and nuns. It was a great honor and privilege, as most people never get that opportunity. Instead, the visitors filed by a window and look into the room of the beautiful girl in a coma. My daughter relayed what happened to me.

Apparently Katelin went right to Linda Santo, which was unusual because she was normally shy and would only go to family members. She was just over one year old. Lisa was holding Katelin when she suddenly leaned down to go on the bed. Lisa told her, "No, no, honey" Linda Santo said, "Let her go.". Katelin crawled up and hugged Audrey who was sleeping. She opened her eyes, and she and Katelin seemed to communicate. One of the priests blessed Katelin with the oil coming from the religious statues in Audrey's room.

The statues at Audrey's weep blood and oil and they reportedly turn and face the tabernacle. There is a tabernacle in her room through the permission of Bishop Flannigan whose consecrated Host bled at Audrey's. He has since passed away. Audrey herself is before the tabernacle twenty-four hours a day, seven days a week. Visiting this child is an intensely Eucharistic experience.

Lisa and Katelin brought a gift for Audrey, the little girl has many religious objects, but my daughter gave her a Cabbage Patch doll, which she had put a trache and feeding tube in to show the common bond that Audrey and Katelin shared. I missed that moment, but I have lived it many times in my mind's eye. It was a day of many blessings, a day I would cherish for the rest of my life.

When I arrived at the house, I was led into a small one-car garage, which had been converted into a chapel. I was immediately struck by the sight of oil coming forth from many of the religious objects in that room.

It was a surreal experience where I felt caught between one world and another. Human nature prevailed and caused me to pick up a statue of the Blessed Mother, which was weeping copiously. I looked for an electrical outlet or a pump but there wasn't any! I looked for a reasonable explanation, but found none. As I looked around the room I saw crucifixes, pictures, icons, and statues all exhibiting the same phenomenon. I had heard mention of these extraordinary events over the years but I never expected to witness them in my lifetime.

Lisa and Katelin came into the chapel and Lisa told me what happened in Audrey's room. Oddly I had not missed them or felt alarmed in any way. As Lisa looked around all she could say was, "Oh, my God!" Those were my sentiments exactly!

We were all seated and Mass began. The three priests who concelebrated the Mass did so with great reverence. At the time of Consecration I watched as the ciborium was brought out filled with communion wafers. As the priest did the Consecration the Hosts suddenly were covered with oil! When we received communion we consumed the hosts with the holy oil on them. I remember them tasting perfectly normal.

Our visit was about to transcend to another dimension. When Mass concluded we began the Divine Mercy Chaplet and the priest brought out four bleeding Hosts! It is the only time in church history there have been four bleeding Hosts in one spot and it is the only place in the world where there are four bleeding Hosts!

We were allowed to venerate and kiss the Hosts! There are no words to adequately describe this moment, but I learned something about myself that shocked me. I am a Eucharistic Minister, and I've always professed belief in the real presence of Christ in the Eucharist body, blood, soul, and divinity. As I witnessed the Eucharistic Miracle my response was "Oh my God everything they tell us is true!"

It was then I realized I am a descendant of Thomas. I was both excited and ashamed. I thought of our Lord's great love, and his mercy, and I asked Him to forgive me my ineptness. I also asked him to forgive me for any deep-seated doubts I may have.

Our Lord's words in John Chapter 20 verse 29 came to me "Blessed are those who have not seen and have believed." We hear that often in church, but if we back up just a bit. In John again verses 28 and 29 we hear Jesus greet the disciples with "Peace be with you" and then he says to Thomas, "Put your finger here and see my hands, and bring your hand and put it into my side, do not be unbelieving, but believe". And Thomas answered "My Lord and my God!". Whenever I am before a consecrated Host I always say Thomas' words "My Lord and my God!" We must remember

Jesus loved Thomas and he loves us warts and all. He understands our weaknesses and failings and His love supersedes all. The world is made up of believers and nonbelievers, but there are two kinds of believers, those who believe and have not seen, and those who need a little something to help their faith grow. Is God annoyed with the latter? I don't believe so, these are His weaker children who need a little extra spiritual fertilizer. He does give us that fertilizer. In the parable of the barren fig tree Luke, chapter 13 verses 6 through 8 Jesus says "There once was a person who had a fig tree planted in his orchard. When he came in search of fruit on it, found none. He then said to the gardener, for three years now I have come in search of fruit on this fig tree but have found none. Cut it down. Why should it exhaust the soil? The gardener said to him in reply, "Sir, leave it for this year also, and I shall till the soil around it and fertilize it. It may then bear fruit in the future. If not you can cut it down." How many times does Jesus cultivate and fertilize us that we too may bear fruit?

My dear friend Mary Roth once said to me, "Dawn, wouldn't it be great if we received a report card from God to let us know how we are doing! "

Maybe we do, in the form of rosaries turning gold, the miracle of the sun, or bleeding hosts, and weeping statues. Maybe it's the peace we feel while in prayer or the joy we feel amidst great suffering, or the healing of a loved one. Perhaps these things are our report cards, or maybe they are the physical, and spiritual manifestations of our Lord's love. Could these not be the fertilizer to make our Faith grow? Could these not be another way God speaks to us? His message is simple, your prayers are heard, and you are loved. "Do not be unbelieving but believe." When the priest holds up the consecrated Host we should all respond as Thomas did "My Lord and my God."

Thank you Lord for the Eucharist, your most precious gift.

As I watched the priest return the bleeding Host to the tabernacle, I realized I had witnessed something very special. I was aware of a change in myself as I was filled with great excitement. It is an excitement that remains always with me, and the Eucharist brought it about. I was also filled with joy, and peace, and an urgency to evangelize. I had received the Eucharist many times throughout my life, and certainly should have experienced that excitement each time I went to Mass. I cannot tell you why knowledge of Christ's presence in the Eucharist came to its fullness at Audrey Santos that day. It just did. As I have stated I always believed it. I could recite to you like a good baby boomer answering from the Baltimore Catechism. I accepted it but on April 2nd 1997, I knew it and understood it. I truly experienced the reality of Christ's presence, body, blood, soul, and divinity.

There were other gifts that day as well. A Host, which was found in the tabernacle of Audrey's room on Good Friday, was brought out in a Petrie dish. It was partly congealed and smelled very sour, scientists had investigated it and found it to be gall!

Many people in the room experienced the gift of roses. It is the gift reportedly from the Blessed Mother signifying her presence. It is very strong and quite beautiful. Several women in the room experienced it though Lisa and I did not. There are many gifts given for particular reasons and many graces given which are as individual as the persons who receive them. I felt blessed to have experienced so much in this humble home where Heaven paid a visit!

As we were gathering our things to leave an older gentleman came up to me and said, "You know I went all the way to Akita, Japan and the statue of the Blessed Mother was not weeping. I have seen at least 25 statues weeping blood or oil here! This is the spiritual Disney World!"

Unfortunately it is individuals like this that give spiritual pilgrimages a bad image. There are those who travel all over the world to "see" the supernatural. I have a problem with this, and I think it is wrong. A pilgrimage should always be made in the spirit of faith, and prayer should be the central part of it — not the supernatural!

Linda Santo came over to us to say goodbye and wish us well. She asked if we would like a picture of Audrey and when we said yes she took Lisa's camera and went back into the house.

My mother always told me good things come in small packages. Linda is very small, it's hard to believe she's able to hold an ocean of faith in that little body, but somehow she manages. She is courageous, kind, and spiritual. I feel privileged to have met her, and honored to have her share her home and her daughter with us. Of all the things I witnessed that day I think the thing, which touched me the most was the faith that lives in that house. No one leaves there without faith, Linda sees to that!

As we drove home it grew very dark. I do not remember seeing the moon, but plenty of stars! My daughter pointed to something in the sky, which appeared to be following us. At first I thought it was a shooting star than I realized it must be a comet, Hale-Bopp.

We talked about our trip and Lisa told me several people came up to her at Audrey's, and said Katelin would be healed. She asked me if I felt she would. I told her I hoped for it, and I would continue praying for it. We were both very happy we made the pilgrimage, and we both had high hopes for Katelin.

Chapter Sixteen

Home

$\mathscr{M}$y husband greeted me with a kiss and a long hug. He wanted to hear all about the trip, and he seemed most relieved to have us home safely. It was late, and I felt it would be better to talk after a good night's sleep. Sleep did not come. I was still excited and overwhelmed with a great urgency to share my experience with others. I wanted everyone to know Jesus, how I had come to know him. It was the excitement of a child waiting in great anticipation. It was an excitement that would, in fact never leave me.

The next morning I spent a lot of time on the telephone with family and friends, sharing my experiences at the Santo home. When my husband came home from work we talked at great length about my visit to the Santo home. He listened politely and then said, "Don't you think you should be careful who you tell this to. Not everyone will be open to it, and frankly some people may think you're crazy."

I was hurt by his reaction, even though I knew he was just trying to protect me. I told him to deny what happened would be to deny God. I did not feel I could do that no matter what the cost. He said he wasn't asking me to deny it, just to be prudent. It was reasonable advice, which I did not follow. I did not wish to be disobedient I just wanted everyone to feel what I felt. I had such a strong Eucharistic experience and a great desire to share it. I knew the real presence of Christ in the Eucharist is a stumbling block for many Catholics and I felt my witness to what I experienced in the Santo home would give affirmation to what our priests tell us. I thought my story, presented as a journey of faith, could open many hearts to Jesus. I prayed to be a simple and humble "fishermen" for Jesus and offered my services to Him.

My first presentation took place April 9th 1997. A group of women from the Ladies of Charity were invited to my home to view the tape and hear my witness talk. I made banana bread, and several other snacks. The ladies were able to enjoy real and spiritual food. They seemed sincerely interested and I was pleased with how well the evening went. As the last lady walked out the door I was already planning my next presentation.

The next group was a group of young women brought to me by Donna Strom. She is the mother of four young children and a devout Catholic. She sings in the folk group at St. Gregory's Parish and was very interested in my journey to Audrey Santo's. Week after week she would call me, and tell me she had more people who wanted to see the film, and hear the story. I was thrilled with Donna's sincere enthusiasm. Her spirituality was infectious, and she was an avid crusader for Christ.

After a few weeks I asked her "Donna, where are you getting these people?" To which she replied, "Don't worry, you just keep having the presentations and I'll get the people!"

We bonded well and a partnership developed soon it would grow into something more. The hand of God was already upon us, working through us, but we were in our infancy and did not yet recognize this as part of His all encompassing plan.

Donna was a Tupperware distributor, and I could not help making the correlation of how our presentations were much like a Tupperware party, but we were keeping faith fresh!

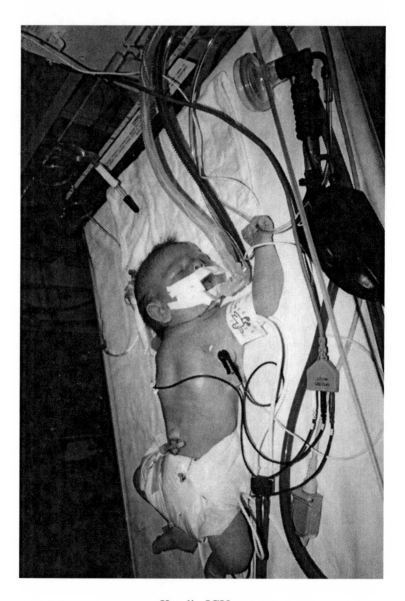

Katelin ICU

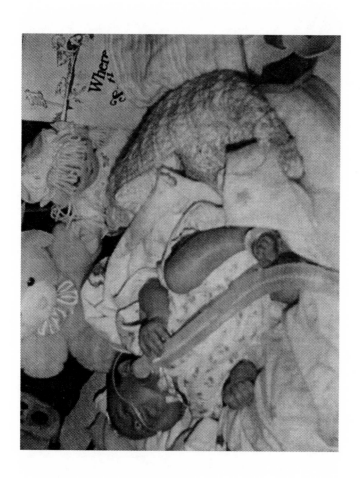

Katelin ICU

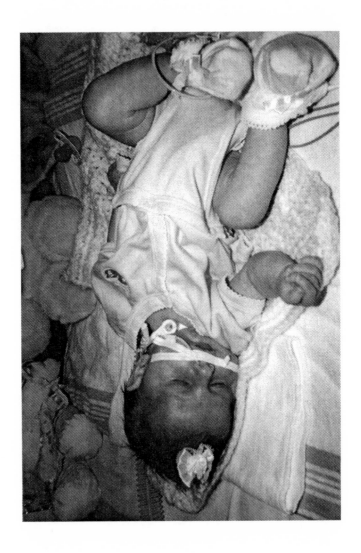

Katelin ICU

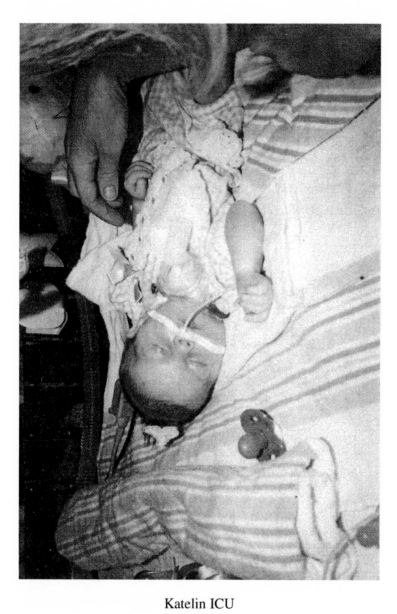

Katelin ICU

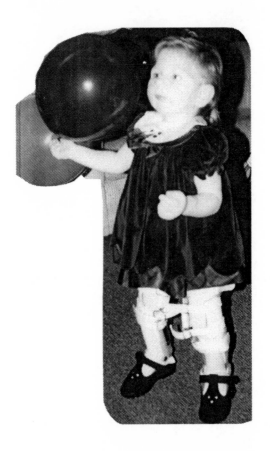

Katelin with her Braces

Katelin beginning to improve

Katelin leaving Children's Hospital after having
her trache removed on April 22, 1998.

Fr. Ted Jost with Mary Cormier preparing to have
Mass at Audrey Santo's

The McQuaid family, from left, Katelin, Lisa,
Pat, Shane and baby Conner.

Audrey Santo

One of the four bleeding Hosts at Audrey Santo's

"The Ladies of the Lord" standing from the left
Mary Roth, Lucy Longobardi, Kathy Deakin,
kneeling Linda Burke, Dawn Curazzato, and
Donna Strom.

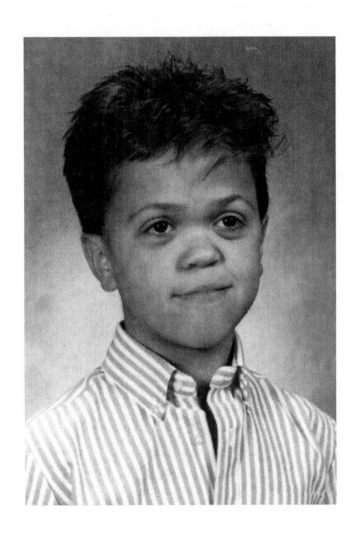

Mike Wachowicz

Seated from left my son Joe, my husband Sam,
myself, my mother Ginger, and my father Milo.

From left Dawn Curazzato, Lucy Longobardi and
Fr. Jim Ciupek at Christ the King Church in
Worcester Mass.

Msgr. Richard Nugent on Apparition Hill in
Medjugorje.

Chapter Seventeen

The Baptism

$\mathscr{I}$ wrote the Dominican nuns about my trip to see Audrey Santo, and about my presentations. They were very encouraging. I gave them an update on Katelin's condition, and asked them to please continue praying for her and my daughter's family. Katelin was making less frequent visits to the hospital and she was learning sign language. She no longer needed the splints on her hands and seemed to be using her hands in a normal fashion. They were little improvements, but we were very grateful for them.

When Katelin was in intensive care I called my parish to see if one of our priests could go up to Children's Hospital and baptized her in case she did not live. I was advised the hospital had a priest who would do that.

I mentioned my concerns to a woman at church who promptly told me she knew a priest who would do it if I picked him up and drove him to the hospital. I was overjoyed! The woman's name was Maria Tupay, and we had a very interesting first meeting.

I would see her at morning Mass but I had never met her or spoke with her. One day after Mass, she presented a Medjugorje medal to me and placed it in my hand, she said, "You are expecting a baby soon, you will need this." I was quite taken back, as my daughter was indeed pregnant with Katelin and I did not know this woman. I thought it was very odd. A few months later Katelin was born with many handicaps, and I remembered that encounter with Maria, and what she had said.

I went to Mass everyday hoping to see her, but she was not there. I did see the woman who walked Maria up to communion, and decided to ask her how I could get in touch with Maria. When Mass was over I went up to the woman and said "Excuse me, but where is the blind lady you some-times lead up to communion?" She said, "Oh, you mean Maria Tupay, she's not blind, she suffers from my Myasthinia Gravis. Here is her phone number."

When I finally reached Maria I found her to be very charismatic and unlike anyone I had ever met. She is an extremely religious person, quick to listen, and eager to help. I told her all about Katelin's problems, and she shared the loss of her young son to leukemia with me. We both cried. I was touched by her deep sincere faith even amidst this tremendous loss. I asked her how she knew I would need that Medjugorje Medal and she said she really did not remember what she had said to me. "But you must!" I insisted. She told me she sometimes gets "feelings" about peo-ple, and she believes the Holy Spirit directs her to console those in need.

I had never met her before, in fact she belonged to a different parish but she came to my parish during the week. Not many people knew Lisa was pregnant. It was all very strange, but a close friendship grew that exists today. Maria also became my teacher in a Bible study class where I learned a great deal. She is a powerful prayer warrior and I consider her a gift from God also.

Maria insisted I call her friend, Father DiGiulio, and have him baptize Katelin immediately. He agreed to do it and I picked him up at St. Aloysius on Cleveland Drive. As we drove to Children's Hospital I filled him in on Katelin's condition. He asked what parish I belong to and I told him St. Gregory's. He told me it was the largest parish in western New York. I proceeded to tell him we had 17,000 people and it was a very busy parish. It was quite a challenge for our three priests and one deacon to minister to so many people, but they were very talented hardworking men. Then I asked Father DiGiulio how many priests were at his church. He said, "Just me." I got very quiet. Here was a priest I had never met, from a parish I did not belong to, who was going to Children's Hospital to baptize my daughter's baby. It was a very humbling moment and I felt a deep love and admiration for this man.

When we got to the hospital we went up to NICU and I introduced Father DiGiulio to Lisa and Patrick. He then baptized Katelin and began praying over her. After a little while Lisa turned to me and said, "Mom, what is he saying?" Father DiGiulio was praying in tongues, an ancient language described at Pentecost. It was the first time we had experienced it! When he was finished I drove him back to his parish. I had a pie, and other baked goods, as well as a donation to give him. He told me he would accept the baked goods, but he refused the donation. I told him I truly appreciated his kindness to Katelin and our family, and I wanted him to take the donation and use it for his parish. He still refused so I hid the check in the pie box. I gave him a hug and thanked him. As we said good-bye he turned to me and said, "God speaks to us through dates and nature."

With that, he turned and walked into the rectory. I thought about his remark as I drove home. In fact, it was that remark which made me think about the events at Audrey Santo's. I saw the EWTN tape on Good Friday. Lisa saw the video on Easter Sunday. We were at the Santo's home between Easter and Divine Mercy Sunday. Lisa's birthday fell on Divine Mercy Sunday that year. The Host bled on June 5th my mother's birthday, and that made me wonder if Katelin's birthday had any religious significance. By the time I got home my curiosity was really peaked and I rushed over to a religious calendar and looked up Katelin's birthday. I almost couldn't breathe as I looked at the date! Katelin was born February 11th, the feast day of Our Lady of Lourdes. Lourdes is a place of healing, and that was the moment I knew Katelin would be healed.

I continued to have presentations, but one in particular was very inter-esting. I was having a group of Protestants to my home, and I was quite excited about the opportunity to share my "journey of faith" with them. When my husband came home from work, I told him about the group coming over that evening. He did not share my enthusiasm. He said, "Isn't it enough you have the Catholics, now you're having these people who do not believe what we do!" I answered, "Sam, it's a story of faith. It's for everyone! I tell it from a Catholic perspective, but it is for the glory of God, and I'm sure that comes through."

He told me he wasn't going to stick around for this one. We talk about ecumenism yet there's still so much fear in sharing with other faiths. We all need to open our ears, and our hearts, and love each other as Jesus asked us to. I don't know what my husband thought was going to happen but it was wonderful! When it was over a woman came up to me and introduced herself as an Episcopalian minister she said, "I believe I expe-rienced a miracle here tonight". I never asked her to expound on that. We just hugged and she left. Then a man named John who was an Evangelical came up to me and said, "You know these signs and miracles are nice, but you don't need them." He then held up his Bible and said, "Everything you need is right here!"

He is absolutely 100 percent correct. I never argue that point, however I did have something to say. I told him if signs and miracles were not important they would not have been such a big part of Our Lord's min-istry. In fact in John chapter 14, verses 12 through 14 during the last sup-per discourse Jesus says,

"Amen, I say to you, whoever believes in me will do the works that I do, and **will do greater** ones than these, because I am going to the Father and whatever you ask in my name, I will do, so that the Father may be glorified in the Son. If you ask anything of me in my name, I will do it."

Jesus tells us how we can tell good from evil in Luke's Chapter 6 verses 43 through 45. A tree is known by its fruit. "A good tree does not bear rotten fruit, nor does a rotten tree bear good fruit. For every tree is known by its fruit."

Nowhere in the Bible does it say that when Jesus dies there will be no more miracles or signs. For some reason the supernatural strikes fear in many people. Certainly apparitions and supernatural phenomenon call for caution. When the church approves of such happenings, as in Fatima and Lourdes, you are not called to believe. Rather, they are called tools of the faith, and the Magisterium has found nothing contrary to the teachings of the church. All public revelations stopped with the death of Jesus, anything that happens after that is called private revelation, even if it occurs and is witnessed by 70,000 people, as was the case in Fatima with the miracle of the sun. Catholics are called to believe church dogma such as the Immaculate Conception, and in supernatural happenings such as the Resurrection, and the Ascension. In fact the five glorious mysteries of the rosary are all supernatural happenings.

I am a gardener, and I find when I use the proper tools my work is easier and my yield is greater. I prefer to use the tools of my faith.

In the Bible Jesus teaches the apostles the only formal prayer we know of and in part it says "Thy kingdom come, thy will be done, on earth, **as it is in heaven**". This tells me none of the angels, or saints, nor the Blessed Mother, can do anything unless it is his will. If the Blessed Mother is commissioned to earth with messages to lead us back to her son, shouldn't we use the gifts of the Holy Spirit; wisdom and discernment, and listen to what she has to say? Certainly there are deceptions and fraud, but if we close the door on all the supernatural for fear of letting evil in, are we not also closing the door in our Lord's face? I chose to leave that door open.

Jesus I trust in you!

Chapter Eighteen

More Suffering

$\mathcal{I}$thought I had suffered enough. My plate was full, so it was some-body else's turn. That's not how it worked! A few months after I was home from Audrey's my face became paralyzed. It was the second time it happened to me so my doctor sent me to a neurologist who ordered some tests. I was told I had Bipolar Bell's palsy and it was very rare. She wanted to put me on steroids and send me for an MRI. I said yes to the MRI but no steroids. I was not in pain, but I had to wear protective glasses, and use eye drops frequently. I also had to tape my eye shut at night in order to sleep. My mouth drooped a bit and I had trouble saying certain words. It was a nuisance, but I didn't let it stop me from fulfilling a very busy schedule. The paralysis cleared up in a relatively short time. After three weeks I was confident the doctor would give me a clean bill of health. That's what had happened the first time, but I had not been given an MRI. When the doctor called me into her office my heart sank as she said to me, "I'm very sorry, but you have had an abnormal MRI. It shows you have had several strokes, lesions on your brain and I believe you may have Multiple Sclerosis."

With shock I said, "Multiple sclerosis! You can't be serious! I feel fine. I can't be sick, I have a lot of people depending on me!" She just said she was sorry, and she ordered more tests.

I knew what MS was and what it did. I had seen its devastating effects on one of my neighbors. It was debilitating and progressive. There was no cure. How was I going to take care of all the people in my life who needed me? I was overcome with fear.

When I got home the house was empty and I was glad because I had a good cry. The phone ringing startled me. It was Sister Maureen Fanning from St. Gregory's. She was calling to confirm an appointment I had with her and Father Jim concerning my trip to Audrey Santos. I had forgotten, and I broke down crying telling her the news I just received. She told me she was sorry to hear it and later Father Jim told me they made a bet that I would not show up. Father Jim was the young deacon who had taken my phone call as I set off in a blizzard to go to Audrey Santo's. He had recently become a priest.

When you put your life in God's hands somehow you find the courage to do things you would not ordinarily do. I knew what I had experienced at the Santo home was important and I put it ahead of my trials. I did not know if I would have another opportunity in the coming months to discuss our visit at Audrey's and I believed with all my heart what we had experienced was of God. I wanted to share it with my parish because it was there at St. Gregory's I walked up to the altar after the presentation on Medjugorje and asked to know that peace I saw on the faces of the parishioners who traveled there. I told my story and Sister Maureen and Father Jim assured me they would present it to the other priests and get back to me.

Father Jim Ciupek, though young, was a very sincere and devout priest. He said the rosary with parishioners many times after Mass. After my appointment with him and Sister Maureen he told me if I was having difficulties in seeking answers perhaps it would be a good idea to go before the Blessed Sacrament. He asked me if I went to Eucharistic Adoration. I was embarrassed to tell him I was not familiar with it. Father Jim told me when you visit Jesus for a holy hour you receive many gifts and graces. He told me other than the Mass it's the greatest thing one can do! My daughter's church, St. Christopher's, had adoration every Tuesday. I decided to go the following Tuesday. Being Irish, and always looking for the pot of gold at the end of the rainbow, my first encounter with Jesus in adoration went something like this,

"Hi Jesus, it's Dawn, I'm here to collect those gifts and graces!"

Then I sat there not really knowing what to do so I just talked about things that were troubling me and I told Jesus I would like to know Him better, that I might love Him more.

I noticed how quiet it was and how very peaceful. Though I was a little uncomfortable because it was new to me, I liked it. The Host was in a monstrance just like the one that held the bleeding host I venerated at Audrey Santo's. I knew I would be back and as I was leaving there was a table with free pamphlets. One was called "How to do Holy Hour." I took it home, read it, and I have been going to adoration ever since. Sometimes I go four or five times a week. I pray, I meditate and I talk to God as I would to a friend. I ask for a lot, I ask for miracles!

Chapter Nineteen

Tests and a Touch of Heaven

The neurologist wanted more tests done to confirm her diagnosis. She ordered a spinal tap and evoked response test. I went to the library and looked up each test. I did not like what I read about the spinal tap so I told my doctor we would not be doing that one. She also set up an appointment for me to see a heart specialist to find out where the strokes were originating. If it was not from my prolapsed mitral valve than I had to have my carotid artery checked. I was annoyed and afraid because I didn't have time for all these tests when my daughter needed me so badly. I did not tell her what was happening to me, because she had enough to worry about. It was getting harder to cover my absences and she was beginning to question me. How could I tell her I was at the hospital or some clinic being tested for MS and strokes? The stress level was extremely high during this time.

One night after a particularly stressful day I could not get to sleep. I went into our spare bedroom and began pacing the floor. My mind was racing and I found myself consumed with bitterness, and I began complaining to the Blessed Mother. I said,

"Blessed Mother, I go to Mass every day, and I say my rosary every day, where is my consolation? Do I look like a Clydesdale? Do I look like I can carry another cross? How am I going to take care of all the people who need me? Can I at least get everyone on their feet before my feet are taken away from me?" Then I cried long and hard.

Suddenly, a very bright light came over me, and out of the light a glittery substance fell on me. It was all over my body, on my arms and on my legs and a great peace came over me. I felt happy in spite of all the turmoil in my life. I said,"Thank you, Blessed Mother!" I did not see her, or hear her, but I knew it was a gift from her because that is whom I was complaining to!

The next day nothing had changed, but my attitude was different. There was a lot of work to be done and I was going to do everything I could for as long as I was able to. That was my plan, nothing fancy, but crying and worrying were sapping too much energy and it sure didn't help the situation.

I called the nuns and various prayer chains and I had myself added to the list. I do not do well at praying for myself. For some reason it doesn't feel right, maybe I feel guilty because I ask so much for so many others, but I certainly knew who to go to for help! No sooner had I put myself on the prayer lists than my doctor called with some test results. They could not find the source of the strokes. Everything looked good. There was more. I passed the Evoked Response test, which was unusual for someone who has Multiple Sclerosis. My neurologist suggested I see Dr. Jacobs who is world-renowned in the area of Multiple Sclerosis. He would be the deciding judge of my diagnosis. It would take four long months before I got to see him. It is the waiting that gets to you!

Physicians Imaging Center of Western New York

atient:	DAWN CURAZZATO D.O.B. 6/28/50	Date:	7/16/97
ddress:	162 SUNDOWN TRAIL WILLIAMSVILLE, NY 14221	PIC #:	1806
hysician:	DR. M. E. ROEHMHOLDT	Exam:	HEAD

MAGNETIC RESONANCE IMAGING OF THE HEAD

IMAGING SEQUENCES: T1 sagittal TR500 TE11, T1 axial high resolution posterior fossa TR600 TE23 pre and post contrast. Proton density TR2300 TE30, T2 TR2300 TE65, T1 coronal of the posterior fossa high resolution TR600 TE23, T1 axial with Gadolinium TR500 TE19.

The T1 sagittal images appear normal. No abnormalities are seen within the brain parenchyma and the paranasal sinuses are normal.

On the T2 weighted images, a poorly defined area of slightly increased signal intensity is seen in the left caudal basis pontis. The lesion does not effect the tegmentum but could be impinging on the exit fibers of the 7th nerve nucleus. Further small focal areas of slightly increased hyperintensity are seen in the mid rostral basis pontis anteriorly and in the right cerebral peduncle. No lesions are apparent in the white matter of the cerebral hemispheres.

On the high resolution T1 views of the posterior fossa, the 7th nerve appears normal bilaterally. No definite abnormalities are seen within the brain stem at this level. The coronal T1 images also appear normal.

Following intravenous Gadolinium, there appears to be a small area of contrast uptake in the posterior left thalamus in the region of the pulvinar. This could be due to a small venous malformation.

IMPRESSION: ABNORMAL MR SCAN OF THE BRAIN WITH THREE AREAS OF SLIGHTLY INCREASED SIGNAL INTENSITY INVOLVING THE LEFT CAUDAL BASIS PONTIS AND POSSIBLY THE RIGHT CEREBRAL PEDUNCLE. THE CAUSE OF THESE LESIONS IS UNCERTAIN AND BOTH ISCHEMIC DISEASE AND DEMYELINATION SHOULD BE CONSIDERED. SUGGEST A REPEAT SCAN AFTER AN INTERVAL AS CLINICALLY INDICATED. THERE IS ALSO A PROBABLE SMALL VENOUS ANGIOMA IN THE LEFT POSTERIOR THALAMUS.

P. Pullicino, M.D. /lw

PATRICK PULLICINO, M.D.

PP/lw

D: 7/16/97
T: 7/17/97

Chapter Twenty

Friendship and Humor

I received a call from Wendy Sittler inviting me up to her summer home in Orillia, Canada just past Toronto. I told her about my diagnosis of multiple sclerosis and she was shocked. She insisted I come up and relax. I told her I had to think about it. I was afraid to leave my family even for a short time. I was about to tell her I didn't think I could make it when she said, Darryl, her husband, would be off with some of his hockey friends and it would just be Linda Fox, me, and her. I still hesitated and she said she had to hang up and would call me back for an answer at a later time. It was near my birthday and I received a call from Linda saying she was in the neighborhood and she wanted to stop by. She told me Wendy was in Florida, watching Darryl play in the old-timers hockey game. I tried to tell Linda it wasn't a good time to stop in, as I had been babysitting all day, and I wasn't feeling well. She promised she would not stay long. When I got off the phone I told my husband Linda was coming over and I said, "I wish she wasn't coming over, I'm upset and depressed, and I just don't feel like talking. I don't want her to see me like this."

A short while later the doorbell rang and I let Linda in. We sat at my kitchen table while my husband read the paper in the other room. We had not been talking for too long when I heard a loud noise coming from my backyard and what sounded like a cry for help. I jumped up and shouted for my husband to call 911 and I ran out in the yard! Linda followed me, and as I walked over behind my garage, I gasped with surprise. There was Wendy Sittler, sitting in the middle of my grandson's baby pool, with a wetsuit on, snorkel and all. She had frog candles floating in the pool and she sang Happy Birthday! What a sight! I never laughed so hard. She

74

knew I loved frogs and she looked like a giant bullfrog sitting in that pool! I always wished I had taken a picture of her that night. I'm sure she is thankful I didn't! Wendy and Linda brought me some "froggy" presents for my collection. They cheered me right out of my dark mood. Both are special friends who stuck by me and always had encouraging words and a heap of laughter. After her prank, how could I say no to getting away for a few days of rest and relaxation. My husband was in on the prank as well, and felt it would be good for me to get away for a few days. He promised he would watch over things on the home front.

In July, Linda and I drove up to Wendy and Darryl's summer home. It is about three hours from Buffalo, which gave Linda and I ample time to get caught up on our families. When we arrived I could not believe how beautiful her home was. Their home was atop a hill and below was lake Simcoe. It was a pristine lake with many beautiful homes along its shore. Wendy took us around and showed us the home and her extensive property. There was a beautiful deck with a hot tub. They had fashioned a man-made natural swimming pool out of the lake. There was a huge break wall, with large rocks that almost entirely enclosed an area near the house. There was a boathouse with two boats in the deep end, a slide, a bridge, which went over the water and connected the property to the break wall, and in the other end were three jet skis. I had never been on a jet ski, but my life was about to get a little interesting!

Darryl was still home. He would be leaving for a mining expedition in the morning. He said, "Would you like me to give you a jet ski lesson before I leave?" "There's really nothing to it." I said, "sure!"

Linda wasn't interested because she had a healthy fear of the water, but she said she would wear her life jacket and ride with Wendy when we went out on our own. Darryl showed me how to start the jet ski and everything there was to know. Then he let me take it out on my own. I loved it! It was exhilarating and for the first time in a long time I found myself letting go and enjoying myself.

I had brought spaghetti sauce up and made us a spaghetti dinner. I also brought some movies for us to watch later. We spent the rest of the night talking, laughing, eating and watching movies.

The next morning I woke up before the others. I went outside, and said my rosary near the lake. I could hear the mournful sound of a loon in the distance. I watched a family of minx play on the lawn. There were butterflies landing on the flowers in the garden and as I watched the golden brilliance of the rising sun on the water for a moment I thought — this is heaven!

If I could draw heaven it would be this place. I was so thankful to be here enjoying the sights and sounds of summer and grateful for these friends. As I was communing with nature and thanking God for this respite I was compelled by the urge to go out on the lake by myself. The waves were choppy, and high, I thought it would be fun to run the waves. After only one lesson I proceeded to take out this fairly powerful machine. I put on a life jacket, pushed the jet ski into deep water, and took off outside the break wall. As I was gunning it, and spinning under the wake I had created, I looked up towards the house. There was Wendy running down the hill in her pajamas waving. I waved back and then I realize she was waving me in. I came into the enclosure slowly and she jumped into the water to help get the jet ski into its place. She said,

"Are you crazy? I can't believe you went out on the lake by yourself in conditions like this! Are you trying to give me a heart attack?"

I said, "No, I just didn't want to wake anyone up, and besides I know what I'm doing!"

She said, "Yeah, right, the blond bomber, wait until Darryl hears about this when he calls in tonight!"

Well, I never lived that one down and when Wendy got a call from Darryl that night she told him, "You won't believe what Dawn did, you've created a monster!"

To which Darryl replied "For God's sake Wendy get the keys to the speedboat before she gets her hands on that too!" I'm coming home earlier than expected!"

Linda and Wendy teased me about it and when my husband called they couldn't wait to tell him either. I actually surprised myself in taking that initiative. I didn't seem to have any fear at all.

Wendy has one unfinished room in her summer home. It is the downstairs bathroom off the deck. She has done something unique. Instead of wallpapering she has every guest autograph the walls. There are the famous and not so famous, but if you look real close you'll see one autograph that reads, "The greatest jet skier who ever lived was here, Dawn Curazzato". There is my fifteen minutes of fame on the Sittler's bathroom wall!

Wendy and I walked every morning and it was during one of these walks that the subject of religion came up. Even though we had known each other since our sons played hockey together, we had never discussed religion. I told her about my experience at Audrey Santo's, and then I asked her where she went to church. She said she watched TV evangelists and received her religious training from TV. I said, "You don't mean like Tammy Faye and Jim Baker?" She said

"Yes I do, I gave money to them." "Oh come on," I said," you helped pay for their damn dog's air-conditioned doghouse!" Wendy laughed, but went on to tell me she believed them because anyone who cried like Tammy Faye and messed up her face with mascara running all over it had to be real!

I stopped laughing because I realized she was serious. She then said some negative things about the Catholic Church and about priests. We discussed her comments in a calm manner and I told her it was not fair to judge the church by the actions of a few. Certainly there is good and bad in all faiths, but I was beginning to see there's a lot of fear and hatred of the Catholic Church. I have been protected and isolated from that sort of thing most of my life, and I realized much can be accomplished on long walks sharing feelings and fears about religious attitudes. I looked forward to our walks and our talks on a variety of subjects. It brought us closer together.

Wendy spoke a great deal about her children. She loves being a mother and loves each one of her children dearly. We talked about the upside and downside of being the wife of a celebrity. If being a mother carried with it celebrity status, Wendy would be in the Hall of Fame!

My little vacation came to an end all to soon. On the last night Darryl came home and we all decided to have one last run on the jet skis. Darryl took out the fastest one. Wendy and Linda shared the next fastest, and I was banished to the slowest one which was still pretty fast. We went all around the lake and had great fun. Darryl motioned that he was going in so I waved him on. When I turned to look at Wendy and Linda, I noticed Linda was hanging over the side, and she looked like she was swallowing half the lake! Wendy was going very fast and did not realize Linda's situation. I slowed down and when I turned their jet ski was empty. I raced towards it and saw two heads bobbing up and down in the lake. I kept circling them as Wendy tried to help Linda back onto the jet ski, but they were laughing so hard Linda couldn't haul herself up. Wendy then tried to get on so she could pull Linda up but that didn't work either. Wendy hollered something to me but I couldn't hear her so I turned off my jet ski in time to hear her yell,

"Will you stop circling us like a great white shark and go get help!"

I quickly raced back to the compound to get Darryl and appraised him of the situation. He followed me out to where Wendy and Linda had spilled and got onto the girls jet ski. He tried to pull them up. He grabbed Linda first because she was shook up, but as he pulled her aboard she got a huge wedgy which made Wendy and I have a fit of laughter. And because she heard us laughing she slid back into the water. Darryl was laughing too and each time he pulled Linda's arms up the same thing happened, her bathing suit turned into a thong! None of us are lightweights so it was a pretty funny scene. Finally Darryl got Linda up and then he pulled Wendy who promptly fell back into the water laughing. He said, "Come on Wendy, I'm exhausted!"

Linda said, "You're exhausted! I almost drowned, your wife almost killed me, and I swallowed half the seaweed in this lake!"

Darryl cracked up and then Wendy said, "Look at Dawn, what good are you circling around like a shark!"

And I said, "What if I would've jumped in to help you two fools and then I couldn't get back on my jet ski? We would all be swimming to shore, and Linda would have to float, because she can't swim! Don't forget I'm the one who brought you help. You ungrateful twits!"

When we were all back on our jet skis we headed for home, and Darryl suggested we all have a nice hot tub. We raced back to the house with me finishing last. Wendy and Darryl started the hot tub while Linda and I went in the house. I asked Linda if she was all right, and she told me she had been very scared, but she was all right now. She put a T-shirt over her bathing suit, and I stuck a few rollers in my hair so I would look decent for dinner. Linda and I went out to the hot tub together. It was very bubbly; Wendy and Darryl were already in. Linda stepped in first, then I swung my leg over but I lost my balance and began falling. Linda was the only thing between me and going under. I instinctively grabbed her T-shirt and fell onto her pushing her under the water. When she came up gasping for air with a look of surprise on her face she said,

"That's it, you two aren't my friends anymore, one tries to kill me on the lake, the other tries to drown me in the hot tub!"

We tried to apologize but every time we did we were overcome with laughter. Darryl tried hard not to laugh but Wendy was snorting, and I had tears rolling down my face. Eventually Linda laughed too, and she forgave us. We try to get together every year at Wendy's summer home, and we always talk about that one special summer where our friendship was cemented in laughter and love. It is one of those special times that live on in your heart and you can conjure it up in the darkest of times to bring a smile to your face. All three of us would call upon those memories as we all faced our trials. Linda suffered severe high blood pressure and an emotional crisis. Wendy heroically battled colon cancer and I went on to battle my own health issues, and fight for my precious little Katelin.

I have often thought how important laughter is to well being. I wondered if Jesus laughed often. Certainly his mission was serious, but he must have laughed sometimes. I searched the Bible for laughter but it was definitely missing. In the story of Zacchaeus, the tax collector, in Luke chapter 19 verses one through ten, I have often thought perhaps Jesus laughed here. Zacchaeus was short of stature, so he climbed a sycamore tree in order to see Jesus who was passing his way. When Jesus reached the tree he looked up and saw Zacchaeus and said to him "Come down, quickly, for today I must stay at your house." Then Zacchaeus scrambled down quickly probably shocked that Jesus was coming to his house for supper. He was after all, a tax collector and a sinner. In my mind's eye, I see him falling out of the tree and Jesus and the disciples chuckling at this man's surprise. Of course this is conjecture, it doesn't say that in the Bible, but I see Danny DiVito in that tree!

So, does God have a sense of humor? I think so. I hope so. Perhaps the answer lies in the abundance of it in his creatures. Some of the greatest comedians of all time have been Jewish. God did make the Irish, and I believe he gave us the choice to laugh or to cry. As I desperately tried to find proof that God has a sense of humor it occurred to me the answer lies with all of us. If you wonder if God has a sense of humor, take a look at yourself in a full-length mirror the next time you step out of the shower! Yes, he does have a sense of humor!

Chapter Twenty-One

Confession

Shortly after I came home from my little summer escape I was notified that my parish priests and deacon wanted to meet with me, at 7 AM concerning a presentation at my church on my journey of faith to Audrey Santo's. I was turned down, but they suggested I get a spiritual adviser to help me with what was happening in my life. My first attempt at finding the right person failed and I became discouraged and disappointed.

I wrote a letter to the Dominican nuns telling them my presentation attempt at my church was turned down and I was disappointed. I told them I had hoped to speak at church as a means to reach more people. I wanted to stand on the spot on the altar where I had asked for the peace of Medjugorje and affirm what our priests tell us. I wasn't feeling well and it was becoming increasingly difficult to have presentations at my home. To make matters worse, Katelin was in the hospital with an infection in the line into her heart, a very serious complication. It would have been very easy to quit at this point.

The nuns wrote back to me assuring me of their continued prayers. They wrote, "My dear, do not get ahead of our Lord. If He wants a bigger door to open for you, He will open it. Maybe He likes your presentations to stay small and more personal."

I couldn't disagree with them. They were always so good to me and always gave me sound advice. It occurred to me; perhaps this setback was for my growth in preparation for what was to come. It was certainly a lesson in patience, which was not a virtue of mine! I felt a bitterness creeping in and I did not like what was happening to me. I was struggling with so many issues and I couldn't cope with the spiritual torment of what was in my heart and the struggle to bring it to light. I went to St. Leo's to confession, and I poured my heart out to my confessor. I told him about Katelin, my multiple sclerosis, and my disappointment in my priests, friends, and certain family members, who abandoned me during my greatest need. I told him my fears, my hopes, and my desire to evangelize. When I was through he said,

"Please come to the other side of the screen."

I said, "Pardon me?" And he repeated himself.

As I took a step to the other side I sat in a chair face-to-face and the priest took my hands and placed them in his. He said,"I'm sorry, I apologize for your priests, and for all priests. What happened to you should never have happened, but let me tell you a little bit about the life of a priest." He proceeded to tell me about hospital visits, and hospice, school and board meetings, and a very overcrowded agenda. He said it is unfortunate, but many priests have been reduced to business managers and that takes them away from the people who need them most. With the lack of priests the challenge of running a parish is much greater.

He helped me to understand and that was the beginning of a healing for me. I could now see my priests' duties in a different way. They had many responsibilities. We talked a little more and I thanked him for being so generous with his time. He asked me to pray for him, and he told me he would pray for my family and me. It was one of the best confessions I ever had and certainly an important one. I looked at the priests name, it was Monsignor McDonnell, and I will be forever grateful to him for his compassion, and for giving me a new understanding of the priesthood.

I thought of our Lord raising Lazarus from the dead. Perhaps we too are raised from the dead through confession. Surely we can be viewed as dead in sin and when we confess we are raised to life again! I certainly felt alive, and this priest made a profound difference in my life, which put me back on the right path. Confession is such an important sacrament, and one, which is very underused. Many people are in line to receive communion, but very few are in line for confession.

A woman I know from church who was aware of my present condition, as well as Katelin's situation, came up to me one day after Mass and said, "Can I ask you a personal question?" I nervously said "sure" she asked, "Why do you go to confession so often? What could you possibly do?" She did not say that because I am a particularly good woman, she said it because she didn't think I had **time** to sin!

The Blessed Mother has requested through the visionaries at Medjugorje, that we go to confession more often, preferably once a month. I try to do that, and I took advantage of this opportunity to witness to this lady. I told her I go to confession for the sacrament, I go for the graces and I go because I sin less. I felt it only fair to now ask her a question.

"Don't you go to confession often?" "No" she answered, "I'm a senior citizen!" Now, I can't wait until I am a senior citizen, but I know of no spiritual discount one gets upon becoming a senior citizen! Here is a very sweet lady, but I don't think she quite grasps the concept of confession, and I don't think she's alone.

The sacrament of reconciliation acts as a dialogue of love, a circuit of grace, which brings us to the forgiveness of Christ through the priest. It brings us back to a holiness, which was disturbed and upset by sin. The forgiveness of sin brings great joy to the soul. Each visit to the confessional should strengthen our value system and make us more Christ-like.

There was another confession I had which was particularly poignant. It was shortly after Mother Teresa died. I met my parents at Blessed Sacrament parish in Kenmore, which is the parish I grew up in. We went to confession, and I stayed to join them at Mass. Blessed Sacrament has been completely renovated and it is a beautiful church. Though the architecture is modern, the statues and artwork are like those in the old churches. It is an interesting and effective way to bring the old and the new together. Monsignor Golombek is an extremely humble and holy priest who takes no credit for the beautiful transformation of his parish. Nonetheless, it is his artistic gifts, which have created the angelic atmosphere. It was he who heard my confession that day.

After I confessed my sins, and was given my penance, I quickly jumped up to leave when Monsignor said,

"Not so fast! Do you know where the crucifix is?"

"Yes, father."

"I want you to kneel down in front of the crucifix, looked up, and read what it says. Say your penance there."

Blessed Sacrament is the only church I've been in that has a picture of Mother Teresa picking up a sick person off the streets of Calcutta. On this occasion Monsignor Golombek had many of Mother Teresa sayings posted throughout the church. When I knelt before the crucifix which was done by a parishioner, and stands on the floor, I looked out, and there, under Jesus' outstretched arms, it said "If you want to know how much a soul means to Jesus look at the cross."

Maybe for the first time I looked into His sorrowful eyes and wept as I said my penance. Jesus laid down his life for our salvation and the enormity of his love consumed me. It took me fifty years, and that moment to "get it." That crucifix with those words is still there. If you should be in the neighborhood, take a drive to 263 Claremont Avenue. Get the key in the rectory if the church is closed, and go in and say a prayer before the crucifix. You won't regret it!

Chapter Twenty-Two

Priests are People Too

$\mathscr{I}$ have expressed my own disappointment with some priests, which came mostly from a lack of understanding of their priestly duties. I would imagine there are many others like myself who place high expectations on our priests. I would also be willing to bet if I took ten Catholics randomly, eight out of 10, would tell me somewhere throughout their life they experienced a hurtful encounter with a priest or nun. Unfortunately, some people leave the church because of one bad incident. I would recommend listening to a tape by Father Benedict Groeschel entitled "When the Church lets us Down." It is an absolutely wonderful tape and a good tool for healing.

With less and less men and women entering the religious life, we are experiencing a shortage. This means more duties pushed onto those already in the religious life, and less availability to us in the laity. As violence, divorce, and abortion rates rise, our need for clergy and spiritual direction increases. This puts a tremendous burden on the clergy. What is the answer? **Prayer.** We need to pray for a stronger calling to the religious life and we need to pray for all those who are already in the religious life. It sounds simplistic and it is, but it works! If everyone started praying faithfully, for more sincere religious callings, and for the strengthening of the religious we have, we would without a doubt experience a change.

We must also pray for families. The single most critical cause of our declining religious vocations is the fall of the family unit. All vocations get their main thrust through the family. It is being destroyed through promiscuity, divorce and abortion. The price we pay is very high not only in our lack of leadership through strong religious vocations but also through immorality, lack of respect of human life and the pervasiveness of the culture of death. Great civilizations are never overtaken by a stronger opponent they fall from within. Moral decay, becoming desensitized to human suffering and the lack of expedient action to help the poor, as well as acceptance of deviant behavior and life styles all lead to serious consequences for a nation. Satan is very busy actively attacking family life on all fronts. Not only has this caused a severe shortage of moral leadership by our clergy, it has also bought about weakness within its ranks. It is easy to fall prey to criticism of a particular priest or nun who may have hurt us in some way but it is far more productive to pray for them. They need our prayers. Healing begins with forgiveness.

I have gone to churches where parishioners have told me, "There is no love here. It is very cold!"

It makes me sad to hear that. Though I have been in churches that have a stark, cold, atmosphere I have never been in one where there is no love. Love is in every Tabernacle of every Catholic Church in the world! We need to remember that. The Eucharist is God's gift of love to us.

I have also met people who say, "I don't go to church every week, but I believe in God. I am a good person. I give to charity and I don't hurt anyone. There are many hypocrites in church!" That's an interesting statement, and many people subscribe to it. I'm sure there are hypocrites in church. What puzzles me is if someone believes in God and considers themselves to be a good Christian why wouldn't they be in church giving thanks and praise to God? Isn't that hypocritical also?

Giving thanks and praise is an important part of worship. It's an important part of being Christian. Yet, we live in a world where thank you has become obsolete. We have all seen columns in newspapers and magazines from people of all walks of life complaining about not receiving a thank you for a particular deed. I remember reading one from a grandmother who gave checks to each grandchild for their birthdays and holidays and never received a thank you note from any of the children. She was very hurt. Her advice from the columnist was, "Stop writing checks Granny until your grandkids learn some manners!"

"Thank you" is a simple phrase that does a lot. It brings joy, satisfaction, and makes a person feel good. If someone does something nice for you why wouldn't you want to acknowledge his or her kindness? Your thank you is perhaps the only confirmation letting a person know their gift has been received.

On the other side of the coin are the people who say, "I never do anything to get something in return. I don't need a thank you for what I do out of the goodness of my heart."

That surely is an admirable statement, but in my experience the people I know who make such statements should stop after the first four words of that sentence. There are exceptions but very few. Perhaps they are not looking for something in return, but a thank you is a gracious acknowledgment for someone else's generosity and kindness. Those words should be used abundantly!

I had occasion to send a particular person at my church cookies and a book I thought he might enjoy. He wasn't in his office so I left it with his secretary. I never heard anything from him and I began to wonder if he had received my gifts. This same person was very aware of my present health condition and of Katelin's and my daughter's situation as well. I decided to write him a note expressing my disappointment. In it I told him without some sort of acknowledgement how was I to know the gift had been received? That note got acknowledged!!

He said he didn't know what to say about his oversight in thanking me for my gifts, but he certainly didn't **have to prove** he cared!

I was shocked at the nasty tone of his response. I found it contrary to all I knew about him, and what he represented. I believe he did have to show he cared, we all do, by the example of the Good Samaritan. If you consider yourself a Christian than you are called to care!

Our priests always teach us to give thanks and praise to the Lord. It is good to give thanks and praise! They also tell us to look for Christ in everyone we meet. If someone does something nice for us should we not thank the Christ in that person?

As for people who leave the church because they feel slighted or hurt I would like to paraphrase what the great Bishop Fulton Sheen once said. No one has ever left the Catholic Church to get more holy. They left because they were angry with a priest. They left because they did not like confession. They left because they did not want to go to church every Sunday, but they did not leave to get more holy! I think that statement says a lot. Stay and pray!

Chapter Twenty-Three

Troubled Waters

Katelin recovered from the infection going into the line in her heart. Where at seven months old she was not thriving, and remained at her birth weight of seven pounds four ounces, now at almost two years old the hyper alimentation made her heavy and puffy. Katelin's deafness was alleviated by the insertion of tubes in her tiny ear canals. It is difficult to test a baby's hearing, and Katelin had to go into the hospital on two separate occasions because testing had to be done in a sleep induced state, and brain waves were noted. She had begun to walk at a-year-old, but she fell a lot. After x-rays and some tests were taken we were told that Katelin needed to wear heavy leg braces. She did not like them at all and cried a lot. Still, she was determined to play with her brother and in a short time she was getting around nicely. Katelin did not like when people stared at her, and my daughter was upset by it too. All the tubes were hidden under clothes and even the trache could be somewhat hidden, but the heavy braces could not. When people would talk to Katelin she answered in sign language, because the trache made it impossible to speak. Her nurses were trying to teach her how to talk by using a speaking valve over the trache but she did not tolerate it well. Her visits to the hospital and her surgeries were now in the double digits. The fear always loomed that we could lose her. To date the longest anyone had lived with hyper alimentation into the heart was eighteen years of age. Katelin had motility problems, and did not tolerate the feedings in her stomach and intestines well enough to keep her alive. She was then fed intravenously but after a period of time her veins collapsed in both arms and the last alternative for her survival was the central veinous catheter, which carried medicine and vitamins directly into her system. Unfortunately, this causes many side effects, one being damage to other major organs. It was ironic that the very thing that was keeping her alive could also kill her. This was the last resort. It was the situation we prayed hardest for to be resolved, and it is what we feared the most.

Katelin also had periodic Bronchoscopes to check the growth of her airway. After one such checkup the doctors were very disappointed. Katelin was still using a trache, which is used in premature babies and she was two years old! This was not a good sign and the doctors told us there was a chance Katelin may needed a trache and a feeding tube for the rest of her life. Lisa and Pat were very upset, as were we all. Katelin was also sent to Boston clinic by Mercy Flight twice a year to see if doctors there could help improve her condition, and perhaps find answers to what was causing it. Lisa flew alone with Katelin and these were very traumatic journeys. The separation from her husband, her son, and her family caused her great heartache, but the need to find Katelin the best care and a cure was her first priority. We always called on many others to pray for Katelin and her many needs during these times. We not only had our Catholic friends pray but also our Jewish, Episcopalian and Protestant friends as well. We were very grateful for the prayers from all concerned.

I continued to write letters to the Santo family appraising them of our situation and asking for their continued prayers. I also prayed to the Blessed Mother to intercede on Katelin's behalf and I had her picture taken to Medjugorje through a lady from church. My husband and I made a pilgrimage to St. Joseph's Oratory in Montreal where many healings had occurred through Blessed Andre as Our Lord's instrument. We placed a picture of Katelin and our petitions on Blessed Andre's tomb. With so many people praying surely our petitions would reach heaven.

Chapter Twenty-Four

A Chance to Help

$\mathcal{I}$continued to do presentations as I felt "Journey of Faith" was important in awakening the faith in others. Even when times were difficult and I felt like giving up I pushed ahead. There were times of anger and despair when I would push all my presentation materials under my bed and say, "That's it Lord, I just can't do this anymore." Many times while telling our story I would pretend I was talking about somebody else, that was the only way I could get through it without crying. Each time I thought I couldn't go on someone would call me and ask me to speak to a group with cancer or a group who had suffered the loss of a loved one. They would say, "Could you please give these people hope with your beautiful witness of faith?" How could I say no? If my story brought peace and hope to others then so be it!

I had missed morning Mass due to a dentist appointment and decided to go to noon Mass. When Mass was over a woman came up to me and asked if I remembered her. She said she had been at one of my presentations and her name was Lucy Longobardi. She asked if I would consider going back to Audrey Santo's. I told her I didn't think so because I didn't want to take the place of someone who might be in greater need since I had already had the privilege of going there. Lucy told me she had an autistic grandson and she wished to pray for him at Audrey's, but she could not drive there. I told her I would mail for some of the miraculous oil, and have it sent to her. Something about that encounter bothered me; in fact I did not sleep well that evening.

I saw Lucy again at church and I thought how nice it would have been if someone had taken me to Audrey's. I saw the same look of pain on her face as I did when I looked in the mirror. I went up to her and said, "If you can get us a date to visit, I will drive you there."

By this time, a book had been written by Thomas Petrisko called, In God's Hands about the life of Audrey Santo. There had been several newspaper articles, a magazine article, and a few things on TV. Later there was an article on the front page of the New York Times, and a segment on 20/20, which literally skyrocketed Audrey into everyone's living room. We had been told there was up to a one year wait after the EWTN program. I wondered what Lucy would be told now that there was a book and more extensive coverage.

When I told my husband I had offered to take Lucy to Audrey Santo's he responded, "Let me see, you don't know this woman, but you are going to drive her all the way to Worcester in our car to see Audrey Santo. Great!"

I told him to quit the sarcasm because I was sure she would not be given a date anytime soon. I was wrong. When Heaven calls, you go and that's all there is to that! Perhaps God was pleased with my gesture to Lucy because some pretty amazing things began happening.

Chapter Twenty-Five

The Real Presence

My appointment to see Dr. Jacobs, the multiple sclerosis specialist, was finally approaching. My first appointment had been canceled due to his leaving the country for a seminar. That meant more waiting and worrying. When I finally met him I liked him. He was tall, pleasant and very professional. He came into the room with my MRI report and all the other test results. He examined me and spoke into a small recorder. When he was finished he called my husband into the room and said, "Well, I don't know what happened to you, but I am pleased to tell you, you do not have MS!"

I was ecstatic, as was Sam. We thanked him, but before we left he asked if I would like to join him at a medical conference to study my case. He said it was a large group of neurologists and perhaps if they all took a look they could figure out what happened to me. He said my case was most unusual. I said yes, but as Sam, and I got into our car to go home I said, "You know Sam, I'm sick of doctors and tests and I don't need to know the answer. All I need to know is I'm all right. I'm not going!" As it turned out he never called me to go to the seminar, but he sent a notation to my primary doctor to test me for Lupus and several other immune deficiency diseases. I took a sabbatical. I wanted to enjoy the moment, bask in the sun and smell the proverbial coffee. For so long our lives had been a series of doctors, hospitals and tests. I needed a break. Why should I go looking for trouble, I had enough. Some people might find that decision reckless or foolish, but I'm comfortable with it. I thank God and the Blessed Mother for hearing my prayers and treating me with such generosity. I now concentrated completely on Katelin and I asked Our Lord

91

for a miracle for her and I promised I would spend the rest of my life spreading His word and declaring His works. That was part of the promise I made a long time ago in my car on John James Parkway! A promise is a promise, and I intended to keep mine no matter how many doors slammed in my face. "Ask and ye shall receive, seek and ye shall find, knock and it will be open to you." Matthew Chapter 7 verse 7.

Several of the doors which would not open to me, were closed because of my witness to the bleeding Host. One priest told me, "Just because you saw a bleeding Host doesn't mean it is of God." This confused me, because the bleeding Host I witnessed was a consecrated Host. I am taught and I believe, that it is the Body, Blood, Soul, and Divinity of Jesus Christ. If it is not of God, then who? Science cannot explain it. There is only good, and evil, and if this manifestation is not of God, who is all good, then am I to believe Satan would be allowed to manifest himself in this way using the precious body of our Lord? I was having such trouble trying to understand this roadblock. I was so sure I stood before God at Audrey Santo's and if I listened to my heart, it also confirmed this. I realized how little I knew about this phenomenon of bleeding Hosts and if I was going to speak about it in my presentations, I needed to learn more about it. I certainly did not wish to mislead anyone.

I went to Father Jim Ciupek and told him my dilemma. He recommended I go out to Christ the King seminary in East Aurora, and use their library. He said I would find what I was looking for there. I found several books about Eucharistic miracles. One, which was called Eucharistic Miracles by Joan Carroll Cruz, was particularly informative. Indeed there have been such miracles throughout church history in Spain, Italy, Germany, Czechoslovakia, Portugal, Belgium, and many other places. Perhaps the most famous is the miracle of Lanciano, Italy. It took place in 700 A. D. after a priest, who had recurrent doubts about the changing of the bread and wine into the body and blood of Christ, spoke the solemn words of consecration with disbelief. The Host suddenly changed into a circle of flesh and the wine transformed into blood.

This miracle underwent scientific scrutiny and a detailed medical and scientific report was submitted on March 4th, 1971. It stated that the flesh was striated muscular tissue of the heart wall, having no trace of preservatives to prevent it from decaying. The flesh and blood was human origin, and was the same blood type- AB.

It is the same blood type that appears on the Shroud of Turin!

I had been reading quite a long time and removed my glasses to meditate and hopefully absorb what I had read. I was thinking it was the Blessed Mother who gave our Lord his physical nature, so the AB blood must have been her blood type. It was reasonable to assume her blood ran through His body if the Holy Spirit begot our Lord. It was interesting that the blood type at Lanciano and on the Shroud of Turin were both AB, the rarest of blood types. Just when I thought I had figured it all out I looked down at the page in the book that I had been reading about Lanciano, and I saw the blood type transposed. This is what I saw AB-BA —— Abba, Father!! I don't believe I thought of it on my own; rather it was given to me. I do not think that way, and at that time I was not familiar with the word Abba. It was a word I sometimes heard at Easter, certainly not a word I used, or thought of at that particular time. What does that mean? Maybe it was a sign, or affirmation, that I was moving in the right direction, but I was not supposed to "figure" anything out, just accept it. The transubstantiation is a mystery which we must embrace with our hearts not our minds. Why do Eucharistic Miracles happen? We already spoke about Thomas and his descendants and it would be redundant to go over it again. Let it suffice to say it is a gift from our Lord to help us believe in His real presence. The message is always simple, it only becomes complicated when we intellectualize. Very often the more intellectual a person is the less spiritual he is. The relics of the miracle of Lanciano can be seen today in the church of St. Francis, Lanciano, Italy.

Chapter Twenty-Six

A Step Out in Faith

With my MS behind me, in my continuous search to know our Lord better, I found my burden growing lighter. I didn't know how long the road ahead was, but I knew my journey would be easier if Jesus was my companion. Katelin was always on my mind.

One day when I was at my daughters home helping her with the children we heard laughter. It was Katelin! I said, "Lisa, how can she laugh with the trache in?"

Lisa immediately scheduled another bronchoscope. When the day arrived we all sat anxiously in the waiting room. The doctor came into speak to us with a puzzled look on his face. He said, "It's only been a few months since we told you there was no growth at all. This is such a surprise, I don't understand it, but I think she's ready to have the trache out!" We were filled with joy. Katelin was scheduled to have the trache out on April 22nd, 1998, years ahead of schedule!

After calling my parents and other family members I sat down and wrote a letter to Sister Mary Mystery of the Dominican nuns. I thanked her and all the nuns for their continued support. I wrote, "Sisters, isn't it wonderful the first part of the miracle is about to happen! Thank God and his Blessed Mother!"

In a short time they wrote back saying "We are so happy for you, and for little Katelin! With you, we thank God, and our Blessed Mother, while praying that all goes well with her when her trache is taken out. **Our Lady does not do things by halves**, so we know all will be well, and God willing, get better and better."

I was astounded by their faith, still I hesitated to show Lisa the letter. I feared if Katelin was not completely healed, my daughter's faith might be crushed by false hope. Then I questioned my own faith. If I believed like I profess to, then I was standing at the crossroads. It was time to take that step of faith! I was reminded of a card given to me by Mary Roth, with an inscription written by Barbara Winter,

When you come to the edge
Of all the Light you know
And are about to step off
Into the darkness of the unknown
Faith is knowing one of two things
Will happen, there will be
Something solid to stand on
Or you'll be taught how to fly!

Someone also wrote "Life is not a series of questions to be answered but a mystery to be lived," to which I added "when we live that mystery with faith it becomes a reality." It was time to live my faith.

We are tested many times throughout our lives, and sometimes our faith waivers and we fall. It is during these periods we are strengthened if we turn to God. That is why I call suffering the pupa stage of Christianity. We must suffer before we become a beautiful butterfly. It is with the wings of a butterfly we will spread the nectar of God's word. To know Him we must know suffering too! We must unite our suffering with His that the saving powers of suffering may be bestowed on all those in need. Yes, suffering is a gift, which draws us closer to Christ. It helps us recognize and minister to those in need. One of my prayers is never to forget my suffering that I may recognize it on the faces of others and reach out to console my fellow brothers and sisters. Good fruit does come of suffering.

If our cross becomes too heavy we need only to call out for Jesus. He will be there for us. Read the well-known "Footprints in the Sand" poem and you will understand.

When the day arrived for Katelin to have her trache out. I went up to the hospital with my mother. Lisa and Pat were already there along with Missy, Barb, and Heather, my daughters three closest friends. I thank God my daughter was blessed with very good friends who were supportive and helpful through her entire ordeal. The girls had taken time off from their jobs to be with Lisa and Pat. Barb Colucci was the sister my daughter never had. She has an outstanding devotion to Lisa and her family.

The doctors allowed me to go in along with Lisa and Pat while they removed the trache. It was an easy procedure. The scary part was seeing all the doctors, and nurses, standing by with machines for life support should something go wrong. I asked the doctor how long it would take before we knew she could breathe without assistance. He said 56 seconds. They pulled out the trache, Katelin cried, and there were a few tense moments, she was given a sucker, and for the first time since she was born, she was breathing without any help! She stopped crying, but now the rest of us were crying. It was a special, and beautiful moment. Thank you Jesus and Mary.

I had missed Mass that morning because I wanted to be at the hospital with my daughter. When I got home I went over to the church to pray a Rosary in Thanksgiving. It was seven o'clock at night, and I had the church to myself. I cried and I laughed and shared all the day's emotions with Jesus and his mother. Then for some reason I grabbed the Missal to check the day's readings, and I happened to look at the antiphon, it said,

"I will be a witness to you in the world, oh Lord. I will spread knowledge of your name among my brothers. Alleluia." And after communion in the book it said,

"The Lord says, I have chosen you from the world to go and bear fruit that will last, alleluia."

I found myself crying again, here was my promise to God, and his word speaking right to my heart on the very day Katelin's trache came out! Coincidence or God incidents?

Chapter Twenty-Seven

The Second Trip

Lucy had gotten our day to visit Audrey and made hotel reservations. I was excited about being able to go back and visit, and now I could bring medical documentation to Audrey's mother Linda, to keep a record of Katelin's progress. As the time was drawing near to leave I received a rather interesting call. It was from Father Jim Ciupek, who was the young deacon I had spoken to before we drove into a blizzard a year ago. He said he felt called to go to Audrey's with us, but he did not want to hurt my feelings.

"What do you mean? I asked,

He said, "Well, I was a chemist before I became a priest, I have a strong scientific background, and I have a lot of trouble with the supernatural stuff. However, I leave a small place in my heart to be touched."

I said, "Well Father, that's all you'll need." Then I proceeded to tell him what he would experience."

When I hung up the phone, I turned around and there was my husband shaking his head, he said,

"Dawn, what are you doing telling this priest what he is going to see? You haven't been there in a year. You don't know if the statues are weeping or bleeding or if the Hosts are bleeding. Why are you taking a priest who doesn't even believe?"

"Sam, he said he feels called to go, who do you suppose is calling him? Perhaps there is a reason God wants him there."

This time I did know something would happen, because when Lucy gave me our dates I looked at my religious calendar, and the dates coincided with personal and religious meaning.

When Katelin was born so sick, I invoked the Angels around her, but I wanted her to have a special angel. I was very simple in my selection since everyone knows Gabriel and Saint Michael, I'd go to Raphael, maybe he wouldn't be too busy. I knew absolutely nothing about him. Much later I found out his name means "God has healed". He is the physician of the Angels. He is also the angel of travelers. Our travel day, September 29th is the feast day of the Archangels Gabriel, Michael and Raphael.

The other saint I often pray to is St. Therese, the Little Flower. I happened to be doing a novena to her. The day we were to be at Audrey Santo's for our visit was September 30th the day St. Teresa died.

Our first sign that this would be a special trip came when we checked into the hotel that Lucy had booked. It was the Day's Inn and when we went to check in there was a big picture of Mother Teresa of Calcutta. I called Father Ciupek over and said, "Look at this! What are the chances we would end up in a hotel with Mother Teresa? Come to think of it when was the last time you were in a hotel with pictures of a religious nature? It's unusual isn't it" He responded, "So what's this some sort of sign?"

"You bet it is!" I answered.

Just then a man from India approached us with our room keys. I told him I admired the picture and he told us his sister's friend had painted it. She knew Mother Teresa. He gave us an article, which appeared in a newspaper from India. I told him how Mother Teresa raised the conscience of people and devoted all her life to make the lives of the suffering better. Father Ciupek was no longer laughing. We grabbed some dinner at the hotel and then went to our respective rooms to get a good night's sleep

When we reached Audrey Santo's the next day Father Ciupek went in to dress in his vestments. He would concelebrate the Mass with two other priests. During the Mass the Chalice on the altar filled with oil. The consecrated hosts we received in Holy Communion were also covered with oil. Father Ciupek, who had visited Audrey, reported seeing blood in the tabernacle in her room. He also witnessed statues weeping blood and oil.

It would be a special trip for him and for another woman who came with me, Mary Roth. My daughter was unable to make the second trip and I decided to ask Mary. As it turned out Mary had oral cancer, but she did not know that when we were there. This trip would prove to be a great comfort to her during her fight of this dread disease. A sincere friendship developed. Mary is an intensely religious girl who would become one of my closest friends. We found we had many things in common, and we were able to share things with each other, which we were not able to share with other friends. Mary was extremely generous, she preferred to keep all the good deeds she did a secret. I admired her spirituality, her kindness, and her giving nature. God was granting me yet another gift in uniting me with my spiritual sister Mary.

My friendship with Lucy also intensified. Here is our humorous, "Lady of the Lord! You only need to be with her for five minutes to fall in love with her. She always has a smile and laughs readily. Though she is 69 years old there appears to be no generation gap because of her easy nature. I love watching Lucy at work. She will automatically gravitate toward someone who is suffering, and invite them to her home for coffee. She then puts on a religious video and gives them religious books to read to help them with their problems. I was grateful for my relationship with both of these ladies. God had his hand on all of us and he was about to push us through another door.

There happened to be a film crew from the TV show, "Unsolved Mysteries" at Audrey Santo's. They talked to our little group and I gave my witness about Katelin, and showed some pictures I had of her. They interviewed all of us. We signed release statements and they told us we would be on upcoming segment of Unsolved Mysteries. How very unexpected!

We giggled about it on the way home and we teased Father Ciupek good-naturedly about it. Father, was sitting in the back seat behind me. He kept saying, "That oil, where did it come from?" The poor man was having trouble with what science had taught him and what the eyes of his heart revealed to him.

It was a very special trip. God puts people in your life for a reason, and I was grateful for these people. I was reasonably sure that a bond had been created which no man could break. Father Ciupek has a great love of the rosary and I believe he felt the tug on his heart from the Blessed Mother.

U N S O L V E D
mysteries

COSGROVE/MERKER PRODUCTIONS

Invites you to Watch

UNSOLVED MYSTERIES ON CBS

APRIL 2, 1999.
Date:_____
Please Check your Local Listings

Cone Health #1101

Dawn Carazzato
162 Sundown Trail
Williamsville, NY 14221.

(Katelin was on this program so was our group

This program aired on <u>Good Friday</u>, April 2, 1999 exactly 2 years to the day I was at Audrey Santo's with Katelin. Coincidence or God-incident?

Chapter Twenty-Eight

Channel Seven News Special

$\mathcal{O}$nce I got home I fell right back into my busy routine. I continued to go to daily Mass and to Adoration as often as possible. I prayed always for a miracle for Katelin. I also prayed if the Lord approved of what I was doing, could He please open the doors to some churches so I could reach more people with my story. I also had some people tell me what happened in my family was private revelation, and I should be thankful but I should be quiet about it. I anguished about that, and one day I prayed to the Holy Spirit for help. I reached for my bible and just flipped it open and there was my answer. I had opened to Tobit Chapter 12 verse 7

"A king's secret it is prudent to keep, but **the works of the Lord are to be declared and made known**. Praise them with due honor. Do good and evil will not find its way to you!"

Thank you Holy Spirit!

It's OK to ask the Lord for what you want, but it's best to say "according to your will, Lord." When you least expect it sometimes your prayers are answered in a way you never thought possible.

Within weeks of coming home from Audrey's I received a call from Regina Tiko of Channel 7 news. She asked if Sheila Mahoney could do an interview with my daughter and I concerning our visit to Audrey Santos and Katelin's improved condition. I said I would talk to my daughter and get back to her. We were both a little uneasy because we wanted it to be presented in a truthful and faith filled way. We were not sure if the media would present it in such a way. The name of the series was "Journey of Hope," and it was to be on for three days. Lisa was also concerned about calling Katelin a miracle, because she was still not completely healed. I told her this is where you take a step out in faith. I believed she would be healed from the time I realized what the significance of her birth date was. I told Lisa I would say she was a miracle in progress, and no one had a problem with that. Lisa was also worried how the doctors at Children's Hospital might view the series as a slight towards them because we were putting our faith in the Divine Physician. I told her God uses doctors as instruments of healing too. It is a good thing to pray for them for God to direct their hands in administering care to others. There's nothing wrong with that, it's not God against the doctors, it's God with the doctors. Katelin's nurse was also to appear with us in the interview. When she told her agency she was going to say she believed Katelin was a miracle and was progressing better than anyone had hoped she was told she could not! Funny how we hear a lot of things on TV and all sorts of rights are protected, but heaven forbid someone in the medical field go on TV and use that word miracle. Katelin's primary doctor, Mary Beth Lopat-Winters did go so far as to say they did not know if Katelin's recovery was the natural progress of her disease or truly a miracle, but later in the interview she says, **"We never thought she would progress this far, I've watched her since birth and it's amazing to see her come in, and do the things she's doing!"**

Any worries or concerns we had about the interview disappeared upon meeting Sheila Mahoney. She is a pretty newswoman who handled the interview with compassion and dignity. They taped us for approximately three hours and only used small bits each evening for three days. The segments were probably no more than five minutes. Because so much is cut out and parts can be out of sequence you hope it all comes together. We were pleased with the job Channel 7 news did in portraying "Journey of Hope" with sensitivity and candor.

Sheila Mahoney had an interesting experience herself at Audrey Santo's. She is a newswoman who must be unbiased and objective, yet she was very touched by her visit to Audrey's. She told me she had been trying to get pregnant for nine years. The day after she returned from her visit with Audrey, she found out she was pregnant with twins! God bless her and her family.

Shortly before our interview my husband and I had been out doing some shopping and he wanted to stop at the Media Play store. I said, "Oh Come on, I'm tired, no more stops, please!" He said it would be a quick stop, but I sulked and told him I would wait in the car. Christmas was approaching rapidly and I thought about Katelin. I changed my mind and decided to go into Media Play to perhaps pick up a book and some 'pound puppies' for her. I got out of the car and went into the store. As I walked into the store a man approached me and asked if I would like to make a commercial for Media Play and receive a free gift certificate. My lucky day, I could now get the book and the "pound puppies" for free! Now I felt guilty about complaining to my husband about making this last stop. He laughed, and teased me about making such a stink.

That same week I received a notice that a poem I had submitted was going to be published in a book of poems called "The Great Beyond".

About one month after that I was on the radio concerning antiques. I called in about a Harry James record with Frank Sinatra singing which belongs to my dad, and was worth $550. I could not believe all the people who called to tell me that they had heard me on the radio. It had nothing to do with Audrey —or did it?

Within a three month period of our second visit to Audrey, Katelin would be on an upcoming Unsolved Mysteries segment, our story was on a three-day Channel 7 news series, called Journey of Hope, I was on the radio, I made a media play commercial, and I had a poem published!

I thought being fat, fair, and fiftyish meant gallbladder disease! What an unexpected turn of events. Then I remembered the words of the Dominican nuns, "My dear, do not get ahead of our Lord, if He wants a bigger door to open for you, he will open it!!"

All I ever wanted to do was tell my story in church. TV never entered my mind. When I wrote the nuns I told them all I wanted to do was reach as many people as possible as a means to bring hope to all those who suffer. When I look back now at the opportunity that was opened up to me to reach out to such a large number of people through the media I feel truly blessed. It was much more than I hope for, and beyond anything I could have imagined. The interesting thing is this; I asked Sheila Mahoney what made her call us? How did she get our name? She told me a priest gave her my name, Father Richard DiGiulio, the priest who baptized Katelin so long ago when she was in intensive care at Children's Hospital. A priest who represents God, a God who opens doors to those who knock, those who believe, those who persevere! How humbling! What an awesome God we have! I realized I needed that time before He opened the door for my own growth. I needed time to learn patience, which was not a virtue of mine.

Praise be to Jesus Christ now and forever!

Chapter Twenty-Nine

More Gifts

*G*od was not through sending me blessings. He led me to a man who is nothing less than a "Godsend", my spiritual adviser, Monsignor Richard Nugent. He is a prayerful, kind, humble, priest with a delightful sense of humor. He has also been to Medjugorje 12 times though he does not talk about it, or promote it, he is more than happy to answer any questions about the subject. Mostly he tells of the many hours people spend in Saint James church and what a prayerful place it is. It is a spiritual retreat for him.

When we had our first meeting he listened to my story and genuinely seemed to care. I was comfortable with him right away and after talking with him, I felt my yoke was lightened. As I left him, he said, "My door is always open, you are welcome here."

Those are simple words, but I cried because I had longed to hear them!

Monsignor Nugent is the pastor of St. Bernadette's parish in Orchard Park, New York. It is a large, wealthy parish, which is blessed with two other wonderful priests, Father Ray McNicholas and Father Ron Sajdak. It takes me 25 minutes to get there, sometimes it can take almost an hour depending on traffic and weather conditions. It is well worth the ride, because as soon as I open the church doors, love comes flooding out! You truly can feel it. Perhaps that has something to do with the fact that St. Bernadette's, has Perpetual Adoration – Jesus exposed in the Eucharist, 24 hours a day, seven days a week! Oh what blessings pour forth on that parish beginning with the priests. They are all wonderful and have always made me feel welcomed. I love my visits to St. Bernadette's and if Monsignor Nugent is not around, I pay a visit to the adoration Chapel.

During one of my first talks with Monsignor Nugent I told him of the difficulties I was having in presenting my journey of faith in churches. He said, "Why don't you write a book. When you are an author doors open a bit easier."

I thought. Is he kidding? Look at all the things I have going on in my life. How am I going to write a book? I don't know the first thing about it! In fact I was angry at his suggestion. It seemed such a remote possibility.

Well, Monsignor, here's my book and it is as much for you, as for Katelin. Without your encouragement, and kindness, I doubt I would have attempted it. You planted the seed, and yes, my dear spiritual adviser, I know who is making it grow. Any fruits that come from it will come from the grace of God. I thank you for your patience and your positive direction. You are love personified. I have watched you with others and you treat everyone the same, as if you are greeting Christ himself! You remind me of Santa Claus! No, you are not fat or jolly, nor do you wear a red suit. It has more to do with the twinkle of your eyes! It is a "twinkle" that says you "know things." An inner knowledge perhaps, yet one you share humbly with everyone you meet. It is in your handshake, in your smile and in every deed you do. It is in every Mass you preside over. I feel God's love when I am with you and you have brought peace into my life.

I thank God for this humble, holy priest.

Chapter Thirty

Mission

When you are interviewed for a particular program or you make a commercial you sometimes don't know when or if it will be used. Such was the case with me. In the meantime, I had signed up to do mission at my church. There was a waiting list and I had waited for almost a year. I received a phone call telling me I would be part of mission seven which would be starting in November.

Mission is a faith encounter within your parish community although people from other parishes sometimes join you. It is a Christ based experience guided by the Holy Spirit. It lasts approximately eight days and it is a time of prayer, singing, personal growth, sharing, and fun. There are wonderful inspirational speakers and a chance to participate in many activities, which help renew your relationship with Jesus. I had been looking forward to being part of it for a long time. On the first night of mission I was given a folder by the welcoming committee. As a woman handed it to me I noticed it was a beautiful blue color like the Blessed Mother's mantle, and I noticed two butterflies in the upper right hand corner which also reminded me of the Blessed Mother. Whenever I see a rainbow or a butterfly I say a Hail Mary, it's just something I do! Suddenly the woman said, "Oh you poor thing, what an awful number you have been given!"

I looked at her and then at the folder. I had been given number 13. I told her, "It's not a bad number at all, it reminds me of Fatima!" I guess it could be said it was yet another coincidence!

I looked forward to mission each day but on the third day I hemorrhaged, and my doctor sent me for a CAT scan. I was afraid I would not be able to complete mission and I did so want to go. I laid down for a while after my test and decided I was going to go to mission that night. When I arrived it seemed everyone was staring at me. I thought, my God, they couldn't possibly know what's happening to me, I didn't tell anyone. Then a few people came up to me telling me they had seen our story on Channel 7 news and also the commercial for Media Play. The commercial was repeated many times throughout the year. You see God does have a sense of humor, and I think he enjoys surprising His children. Mission was a beautiful experience, and I was able to complete the eight days. My problem had been caused by fibroid tumors.

Chapter Thirty-One

The Ladies of the Lord

After returning from the second trip to Audrey Santo's, Mary, and Lucy, offered to help Donna and me with our presentations. Churches began opening their doors to us, and we worked within whatever guidelines they gave us. We had been to St. John's in Alden, St. Francis of Assisi, and St. Christopher's. About this time Kathy Deakin, a very spiritual woman joined us. She has a strong devotion to adoration. She was involved in many religious activities, which caused her husband Mike, to refer to her as "Sister Kathleen!" She expressed her desire to join us in spreading the good news. Katelin's story was our platform and after each presentation we would distribute scapulars, blessed medals, rosaries, pamphlets, books, and uplifting handouts. I spoke to Monsignor Nugent about starting a prayer group, and he encouraged me to do so. He told me we must be committed to prayer. I informed him I had a name picked out for my prayer group: "Ladies of the Lord." I had given the prayer group considerable thought, because it is a serious undertaking, but I felt something was missing, and I couldn't quite put my finger on it.

Lucy had a presentation at her home and it was there I discovered that it was not a something that was missing, it was a someone! Her name was Linda Burke. She was an attractive woman who was seriously devoted to Jesus. I liked her immediately and I felt she would be an important addition to "Ladies of the Lord". Though she was very serious about her prayer life and steadfastly brought our Lord's love to everyone she met, I discovered she also had a wonderful sense of humor. She was intensely honest and I valued her opinion in many issues. She was never afraid to speak up for what she believed was right, and she was able to do that in a kind gentle manner. As I can be somewhat of a bulldozer at times, I felt she would complement my personality nicely. She would become one of God's most cherished gifts to me.

Kathy Deakin was a quiet lady but beneath that quiet exterior was a woman with an agenda. She was a whirlwind of religious activity, involved in the religious education program at St. Gregory's, several prayer groups and an avid participant in witnessing to Adoration. She and Linda would often go to nursing homes as "Ladies of the Lord", bringing with them a tape recorder, and rosary tapes to play for the seniors. The social director often told them that the seniors look forward to saying the rosary. Kathy was instrumental in getting "Ladies of the Lord" our own letterhead, stationery and buttons, which we wore at our presentations. She presented many good ideas to aid us in finding resources to operate as a charitable organization. Since we are very small group this was no easy task.

I set up the following format for "Ladies of the Lord" as well as our agenda.

To be a member:
1. Promote the Real Presence and Eucharistic Adoration
2. Witness to the word, and how Jesus affects your life
3. Daily rosary
4. Daily Mass whenever possible
5. Do good deeds
6. Give out sacramentals, medals, rosaries, scapulars, etc.
7. Pray for Our Lady's intentions, the intentions all of the Ladies of the Lord and intentions written in our petition book.

I thought of our motto when I was 30,000 feet in the air. I am not a good flyer, and while my husband and I were on our way home from a trip I began saying the rosary. I find comfort in the act and I find it quells my fears. A woman who was sitting next to my husband took notice and asked my husband if I was afraid of flying. He said, "Oh no, my wife always says the rosary!"

Maybe I never expressed my fear to him, I just assumed he knew. It is certainly beautiful to be above the clouds and be able to get a different perspective. I wondered if this were as close to heaven as I would ever get. Then I wondered how anyone survives a plane crash with people crammed in like sardines, and of course that rekindled my fear. Then three words popped into my head "prayer not despair"! And that became our Ladies of the Lord motto!

I wrote to the Dominican nuns about our prayer group and they suggested a patroness, Blessed Margaret of Castello. I read a book about her life, and thought she was perfect for us. She is the patroness of the unwanted, unloved, handicapped, and the blind. Her body lies incorrupt in Citta di Castello, Italy. The bodies of many saints have been found to be incorrupt. When exhumed they are found to be preserved without benefit of any preservatives. There is a book called "The Incorruptibles" by Joan Carroll Cruz about this phenomenon.

The Carmelite nuns sent me a prayer for the devotion to the Holy Face of Jesus. I like it so much I began using it at the openings of all of our presentations.

"O good Jesus, who has said, 'Ask and you shall receive, seek and you shall find, knock and it shall be open to you,' Grant us, Oh Lord, that faith which obtains all, or supply in us what may be deficient, Grant us, by the pure effect of Thy Charity and for Thine eternal glory, the graces which we need and which we look for in Thine infinite mercy. Amen"

We are set up like the confraternity of the rosary, which means there are no dues, there are no meetings, (except for the core group which consists of 12 women). Members promise to conform to our mentioned membership requirements and unite their prayers with the Ladies of the Lord. You're under no threat of penalty for being unable to do all the requirements but retain the benefits of all prayers united with the Ladies of the Lord. We have a petition book, which all people therein are lifted up in prayer. It is the power of prayer that keeps us going. It is the heart of what we do. When we do a presentation a basket is put out for a "love offering" which we use to buy the materials we give away. Nothing is expected or asked for, as we want everyone to take what we have to give. The donations help offset our expenses and we are grateful for that. There are three of us who do the buying and footwork, most of it is at our own expense. Everyone's duty or offering must come from the heart. It is completely volunteer and I fully expect long after the presentations have stopped we all will still be Ladies of the Lord doing God's will. It's not about our story; it's about Jesus, and using our life experiences to bring others into a closer relationship with Jesus. Each one of the Ladies of the Lord has a "life experience" to share. The ages range from 34 to 70. We have girls who talk about natural family planning and the family rosary. Three girls are dealing with cancer and share their expertise with others experiencing the same. Two girls share the loss of the child with others and all of us promote Adoration, the rosary and prayer. We offer Christian fellowship for every need. What do we do if we get a question we cannot answer or situation we are not equipped to handle? I confer with my spiritual adviser Monsignor Nugent. We get the name and address of the person who asked the question and we mail the answer from Monsignor Nugent to the person. We do not pretend to be anything we are not. We are all very different; our common bond is Jesus and prayer. For me, it is perhaps more. When I lost my friends during my sufferings I was angry with God. I did not see His plan. I would not have had the strength or courage to walk away from my friends, even if they were taking me in the wrong direction. I needed them so badly at that time in my life I was hanging on out of sheer desperation. Their loss was just another devastating blow or that's how I viewed it. Look what God has done! He replaced what was lost with "the Ladies of the Lord". My life is truly blessed to have these beautiful women of faith as my friends. They do not run from suffering, they stay and pray. Thank you Jesus for my friends, forgive me my complaints!

There is another priest I confer with, Father Joe Bertha. Father is a Byzantine priest and an expert on icons. He is extremely knowledgeable and has made himself available for any of my questions.

When he was a young child he had rheumatoid arthritis which was quite painful. A friend of his mother went to Lourdes and brought some water back from the healing spring. Father Bertha's mother gave it to him to drink. He did so and was cured of his condition, which he attributes to the healing water of Lourdes, which was promised by the Blessed Mother. Understandably he has a strong devotion to the Virgin Mary. He also believes this impacted his decision to become a priest.

He was very opened to my story and consistently prays for Katelin and our family. Father Bertha has also blessed every room in our house.

Chapter Thirty-Two

"By Their Fruits You Shall Know Them"

As my family's prayer life increased so did its spiritual gifts. My husband, who was a skeptic and unsupportive in the beginning, was now saying the daily rosary, reading the Bible, and even helping me with my presentations. Where he had always been a good man and a good father, we had our differences in certain areas. Now our marriage was stronger than ever.

My son-in-law, Patrick, who teaches science and at the time of his marriage claimed to believe in a "higher up", but was not following any set pattern of his faith, is now back in church and receiving the sacraments. He and Lisa were teaching Sunday school for a while. Lisa goes to church and confession regularly as well as Adoration. She sees to it that her children are getting a good Christian upbringing.

My parents' prayer life has increased and they go to Adoration often.

My son struggles, but I pray someday he will find peace through Jesus.

Perhaps many people have been touched by Katelin's story, which appeared on television, and in May of 1999, a full-page story appeared in the Western New York Catholic Paper. I had corresponded with Monsignor David Lee concerning the events happening in our family. He is now editor-in-chief of the Catholic paper, and I thank him for his profound wisdom and kindness in sharing our story with so many others. Where many have been touched by it others have not.

There is a parable in the Bible (Matthew, Chapter 10 verses 34-36) where Jesus says, "Do not think that I have come to bring peace upon the earth. I have come to bring not peace but the sword. For I have come to set a man against his father, a daughter against her mother, and a daughter-in-law against her mother-in-law and one's enemies will be those of his household."

I have never liked that one. It upset me. It did not sound like the God I knew and loved, but I have come to know it's meaning. It means there will be division when one chooses God and another does not. Unfortunately this will cause division within friendships and families. Some will turn to God, others will turn away from him. It does not mean that all is lost, it means those who turn from God have lost their way, and are in need of our prayers. When you think a person or certain situation is hopeless, pray. If there is a wall of division, pray for God to take it down brick by brick. It's hard when someone in your own family appears to be against you or a close friend deserts you because you have chosen God. Just pray and let God find a way. Prayer is the answer!

There is another parable I know well too. Mathew Chapter 13 verse 57, "A prophet is not without honor except in his native place and in his own house." Do not go where you are not welcome, shake the dust off your feet and move on. Do good and evil will not find its way to you. Pray for those of little faith and your own will increase. Have an attitude of gratitude! These things I try to do, and I am grateful for the many good fruits, which have come forth.

Chapter Thirty-Three

Science and Miracles

*M*any intellectuals tend to ignore signs and miracles. They simply do not put a lot of stock in them, they are unmoved by them. An intellectual will look at the universe and say,

"I can figure this out!"

The simple man says, "Why? God already has!"

Actually science and religion were very compatible until science divorced itself from the supernatural. There are those who believe strongly in UFOs, but dismiss apparitions as pure nonsense. It is my personal opinion that UFOs are not from another world, but from the nether world. My parents will tell you I have been saying that since I was a child. My father worked at Bell Aerospace, and was a big UFO buff. I never believed in them like he and many others did. Oh, I believe they exist, as the chariots of hell! I say that because people who claim to have had an encounter with them speak of fear. They described the beings as demons, they sometimes smell sulfur, and the encounter is always unpleasant. Sounds like hell to me! Does anyone really believe if there were pieces of an alien ship or alien bodies, the story would not have been in every paper in the world? There are no secrets anymore where there is money to be made. A story like that would generate a lot of money. UFOs sightings have been reported since biblical times, described as flying wheels. If they are from a highly intelligent civilization why haven't they done something about us a long time ago? Perhaps where visions and apparitions of angels and the Blessed Mother are good, UFOs and the like are evil. There are always the forces of good and evil.

Virtually every continent has a visionary or some type of phenomena occurring. There is a weeping statue in Akita, Japan, a bleeding host in Betania, Venezuela, where rose petals rain down from a clear blue sky on the farm of visionary, Maria Esparanza and many pilgrims claim to have seen the Blessed Mother. There are the seven visionaries in Kebeho, Africa; several of whom have been martyred. In Medjugorje, the Blessed Mother is reportedly appearing to six children who are receiving messages, and 10 secrets since 1981. There is Christina Gallagher of Ireland who receives messages, and has the wounds of Christ. In the United States, we have the visionaries in Scottsdale, Arizona, Nancy Fowler in Conyers Georgia, and little Audrey Santo of Worcester MA where communion wafers bleed, and statues weep tears of oil and blood. What's going on? What is a Christian to do?

A Christian should always pray to the Holy Spirit for wisdom and discernment and seek knowledge through Scripture as in John Chapter 14's Last Supper's discourse and John Chapter15 about the vine and its branches. Perhaps it would be helpful to discuss what not to do! I'm sure many people have seen the movie the Ten Commandments. When I think of Moses, I think of Charlton Heston coming down that mountain in all his majesty carrying the Ten Commandments to his people. In actuality, Mel Tillis, should have played Moses stumbling down the mountain. Moses was a bumbler and a stumbler, his brother Aaron was the eloquent speaker.

How about this guy,

"He was a small man, bald, bowlegged, with meeting eyebrows, and a large red hooked nose. He was a citizen of the Roman Empire and was one of the most ferocious persecutors of Christians."

This was St. Paul as described from Ronald Browning's book Who's Who in the New Testament.

God chose these two men to be great leaders even though they were flawed.

When I do my presentations, I hold up a picture of Cindy Crawford, and I say, "This is what's beautiful in the eyes of the world." I then hold up a picture of Mother Teresa of Calcutta and say,

"This is what's beautiful in the eyes of God. This is the beautiful we should strive to be". I then go back to the Cindy Crawford picture and say, "In ten years I will have to change this picture because she will no longer be considered beautiful, the world is fickle. Then I go back to Mother Teresa and say, 'but this picture will remain beautiful forever!"

Maybe some people have met Nancy Fowler, of Conyers Georgia, or John Leary of Rochester, or Father Stephano Gobbi of Italy. Some might say they are not physically attractive, or particularly good speakers. Does this mean they are not true visionaries? We are not to judge the messenger; we are to judge the message!

The best course of action is to let the Magesterium of the church rule on the authenticity of a particular vision or visionary. If the church ruled Medjugorje or Audrey Santo were not authentic, I would be upset, I would be disappointed, but I would obey the church, and it would not change my faith. The whole purpose of apparitions is lead people to God. If you have God in your life it should not matter what happens to an apparition. Controversy in and of itself is not a sign that a particular vision is false. In fact, in the case of Bernadette Soubious of Lourdes, no less than 100 other young women claimed to see the Blessed Virgin Mary! Satan is always close by to create doubt and controversy.

Chapter Thirty-Four

Proof?

$\mathcal{I}$s the shroud of Turin, the miracle of the sun, Eucharist miracles, and statue's weeping oil and blood proof of God's existence? Some say yes, others no. For those who have faith, no proof is necessary, for those who do not, no proof will be enough. Faith itself is a supernatural virtue. It is a key element in healing. Many times Our Lord said, "Go, by your faith you have been healed." Many people who are cured of a terminal illness claim their healings are proof God exists. Certainly, there is a lot of evidence that God exists, but those who do not believe will always discount it. Why should that matter to those who do believe? I was taught evolution in school, but if evolution was true shouldn't we be seeing some new species by now? Animals and creatures of the earth are not evolving they are disappearing!! Every few years it seems someone claims to have found the "missing link" to connect humans to the ape. So far no definite link has been proven.

I find these historical events* far more interesting. In Hiroshima, four Jesuit priests survived who were at the very epicenter of the atomic blast. They were praying the rosary. The same thing occurred at Nagasaki. A group of friars were saying the Fatima prayers, and were at ground zero of the atomic blast. Not only were all the holy men very much alive, they had no radiation burns, and never got cancer. That is a medical, and scientific impossibility! What saved them? Prayer. The war ended August 15th, the date of Mary's assumption, the church the Jesuit priests survived in was the church of Our Lady's Assumption. Coincidence? Or God incident?

On May 13th, 1955, for some unknown reason which historians cannot explain the Soviet Union packed up and left Austria which was the crown jewel in its strategic centerpiece of World War II occupation. This occurred after 70,000 Austrians agreed to pray the rosary. May 13th happened to be the anniversary of the first apparitions at Fatima. When the Communists tried to overtake Brazil, thousands of women stormed the streets and prayed the rosary. For some unknown reason the Communists left.

When Nikita Khrushchev visited the United Nations in October 1960, he boasted the

"Soviet Union would, "bury us!" He took his shoe off and pounded on the podium before the horrified World Assembly. This was no idle boast. Khrushchev knew his scientists had completed their work on a nuclear missile.

Here's what happened. Pope John the 23rd had opened and read the third Fatima secret. He authorized the bishop of Fatima to invite all the bishops of the world to join the Pilgrims of Fatima on the night of October 12 through the 13th in 1960 in prayer and penance for Russia's conversion, and world peace.On those nights about one million Pilgrims spent the night in prayer and penance in the Cova da Iria at Fatima despite a chilly rain. At the same time at least 300 dioceses around the world joined them in prayer. Pope John sent a special blessing to all taking part in this night of reparation. On the night of October 12th and 13th Khrushchev, suddenly left in great haste to return to Moscow. Why?

Marshall Nedelin and the best minds in Russia on nuclear energy, and several government officials were present for the final testing of the missile that was going to be presented to Khrushchev. When countdown was completed, for some reason the missile did not leave the launch pad. After 20 minutes Marshall Nedelin and all the others came out of the shelter. When they did, the missile exploded killing over 300 people! This set back Russia's nuclear program back for 20 years. It happened when the whole Catholic world was on its knees before the Blessed Sacrament, at the feet of our Rosary Queen in Fatima.

This quote is from Revelation chapter 8 verse 10.

"When the third angel blew his trumpet, a large star burning like a torch fell from the sky. It fell on a third of the rivers, and on the springs of water. The star was called 'wormwood,' and a third of all the water turned to wormwood. Many people died from the water, because it was made bitter." The Ukrainian word for wormwood is Chernobyl.

These are just a few examples of the power of prayer, which seem to have altered the course of history.

* Information gathered from <u>The Last Crusade</u> by Thomas Petrisko.

Chapter Thirty-Five

Motherhood, Abortion and Adoration

Katelin continued to improve once the trache was removed. In a short time her heavy braces were also removed and one day she began eating small amounts of food. It was an encouraging sign. The feedings through her heart bypassed her stomach. Our fear was if you don't use it you lose it, and her stomach was not being used. We were told they would try to wean her off some of her feeds. This would be a long process of trial and error.

Lisa and Patrick wanted another child. Some will read that sentence and say they must be crazy to take a chance like that with all they have been through. Others will say what faith they have! At any rate, Lisa did become pregnant, and yes, we all worried because there was no definitive answer as to why Katelin's condition occurred. Was it something inherited, or was it caused by the tumor on her thyroid during her pregnancy? The doctors just weren't sure. The thyroid controls many bodily functions, Lisa was missing half of hers, how would that affect her pregnancy?

The doctors wanted to do some tests to see if this baby had any handicaps. Lisa thought about it, and said no. She said,

"Mom, I have no intention of aborting this baby, so why do I need these tests. I will take whatever God gives me, and if he gives me another sick child, maybe it's because he knows I will love that child and take care of him or her."

I was so proud of her response. She had progressed so far from those troubling teenage years.

Since my daughter now had two children to raise on her own she one day called me and said,"Mom, I'm sorry, I was such a brat and now I have some idea of how much I put you through. I know you always loved me, and just wanted what was best for me. I love you mom." I did not think I would live long enough to hear those words! Lisa never calls me, or her father, without saying "I love you" before we hang up. I am very proud of the person she has become and she truly excels at being a mother. A mother's role is so important.

At the Miracle at Cana, when you look closely, there is much more going on than Jesus turning water into wine. We see His mother Mary asking for a favor, and he replies (John Chapter 2 verse 4),"Woman, how does your concern affect me? My hour has not yet come." I've always thought that reply seemed a little testy for Jesus. Why did he call her woman instead of mother? There is only one other place in the Bible where Jesus refers to her as woman. In John Chapter 19 verses 26-27 when he sees his mother at the foot of the cross he said, "Woman, behold your son." To his disciple he says, "Behold your mother." Is he not identifying her as the Woman in Revelation Chapter 12, "the Woman clothed with the sun, with the moon under her feet and on her head a crown of 12 stars"? What does Mary, his mother say after his terse reply? She turned away from him and says to the servers at the wedding feast "do whatever he tells you" now I'm really confused! It looks like she is ignoring her son, and of course is well aware of whom he is. It seems very presumptuous. Is it perhaps because she knows since she gave her fiat to become the Arc of the Covenant her son will deny her nothing? Is this not the moment we learn Mary will be a great intercessor for all of us? Does Jesus say no to her? Does He not go ahead and change the water into wine? Is this not the precursor to a later time when He will turn wine into his blood? When we meditate on a miracle we usually see more than one thing going on.

I am troubled by the controversy within the church and within the world on the role of a woman. Many say there should be women priests. I say if Jesus wanted women to be priests he would've given testimony somewhere in the Bible about it. I am a simple person, and I tend to look at things in a simple way. God already gave me a great gift; I am the vessel, which brings life into this world. No man ever feels the stirrings of life within the womb. There is no greater honor in this world than being a mother. I don't say it is the greatest job, I think the greatest and most important calling is to the clergy, but there is no greater honor than being a mother. That is why I am also very disturbed about abortion. We dishonor motherhood through abortion. There have been over 32 million abortions performed in the United States, and over 1,273,000,000 worldwide! That is so shocking, and yet many have become indifferent to it. The soul of a nation is judged by the treatment of its people. What judgment will befall us in this culture of death? What can we do to stop this greatest Holocaust of our times?

First of all, don't deny that it's happening, and don't say what a woman does with her own body is her business. Abortion is not a complicated matter, let there be no confusion.

When those two cells meet, life begins. If you do not interrupt them a baby is born. If you do interrupt them, you have taken the life of a baby! It is interesting to note when a child is wanted it is called a baby. When it is unwanted it is called a fetus. Do not be fooled by words that are thrown out to ease your mind. We should all be uncomfortable with what we see happening. You cannot oppose evil and then compromise with it. We do that a lot in this country. We suffer from the paralysis of analysis, so much so we are unable to tell right from wrong anymore. We are so desensitized to sex and violence that many of us who call ourselves Christians never stand up for the afflicted and the downtrodden.

I recently stood against abortion on Niagara Falls Boulevard with Linda one of my Ladies of the Lord, and my parents. I held a sign that said, "Abortion kills children". Some people went by in their cars and honked and gave a thumbs up sign of approval, others hollered obscenities and stuck up their middle finger, but the great multitudes went by and <u>did nothing</u>. These are fence sitters, people who could make a difference, but choose not to. We need to pray for these people for their conscience to come alive that they may once again join the Christian community with their whole heart. Lest anyone think this is not important, here's what Our Lord says about these people

"I know their works that thou are neither cold nor hot. I wish they were cold or hot. So because thou are neither cold nor hot I will spit them out of my mouth." In some translations it reads I will vomit them out! **Do not be lukewarm**! We must also remember "thou shall not kill," means babies as well as abortion doctors!

Perhaps you are not inclined to march against abortion or hold a sign, that's perfectly all right, but you are called to defend the innocent. This can be done in prayer or simply by voicing your convictions when an opportunity arises. For instance at a luncheon, you may be at a table with other women who say they are pro-choice don't be afraid to say, "I'm pro-life" I don't believe in murdering innocent babies. Maybe you'll get the cold shoulder, but you won't from our Lord! In the scheme of things what is more important?

Another very powerful tool is adoration of the Blessed Sacrament. Go there and pray for the unborn. Other than Mass it is the greatest thing one can do. For those who are not familiar with it and what it does I would like to take a quote from the movie "As Good as it Gets". There is a scene in that movie where Jack Nicholson looks at Helen Hunt and says, "You make me want to be a better man." That's what Adoration does. As we sit before our Lord in the Eucharist, He makes us want to be better people. If we become better people, our families become better, our churches become better, our country becomes better, and eventually the world becomes a better place!

Chapter Thirty-Six

Conner, Katelin and God

$\mathcal{L}$isa had a baby boy on May 2nd 1999. The doctors came out and said there's a problem and I felt my heart sink. This time I knew what to do, and I knew I must accept the Lord's will. As happens in our family often enough, this too was a special date. It was the date of Padre Pio's beautification whom my father has such devotion to and whom I had heard about since I was a child. The baby was having trouble breathing, and had some similarities to Katelin, but not nearly as severe. I prayed and put this baby in Padre Pio's care. I prayed for him to get well, and I offered him up to God as a future priest if it be His will. His birth certificate reads Conner Patrick <u>Pio</u> McQuaid". He is an Irishman, with just enough Italian to make him a fighter. At ten months old he seems to be perfectly fine, thank God and the intercession of Padre Pio.

Through all their struggles, a very spiritual and compassionate priest supported my daughter and Patrick. Father Ted Jost of St. Christopher's, who was instrumental in leading Patrick and Lisa back to church and with bringing them into a stronger communion with their faith. He has a great love of Jesus and Mary, and recently became a Marian priest. Father Ted personifies what it is to be a man of God, and we thank him for his kindness, compassion, and guidance. He has also been to Medjugorje and to Audrey Santo's, which were part of his faith journey. He is the godfather of Conner Patrick Pio McQuaid!

At this point in time Katelin sees, she hears, she breathes and eats on her own, and she is in dancing school! Gone are the heavy braces, the tubes in her stomach, her intestines, and her heart. Perhaps the greatest miracle is her mental capacity. When tested recently, not only was she age-appropriate, she was above!! She laughs and plays with her two brothers and most importantly she knows she is loved.

The Bible is the greatest story ever told, the next greatest story is yours. The one you witness to how Christ has affected your life. I witness to you today, that I have neither health nor wealth, but I may be one of the richest people in the world because I have found the pearl of great price and it is the Eucharist. Won't you please join me, and the Ladies of the Lord, in Eucharistic adoration, and giving thanks and praise to the Lord? You don't need an open mind just an open heart. Thank you.

Paradox of Prayer

I asked God for strength that I might achieve
I was made weak that I might humbly obey
I asked for health that I might do greater things
I was given infirmity that I might do better things
I asked for riches that I might be happy
I was given poverty that I might be wise
I asked for power that I might have the praise of men
I was given weakness, that I might feel the need of God
I asked for all things that I might enjoy life
I was given life that I might enjoy all things
I got nothing that I asked for, but everything I had hoped for
Almost despite myself, my unspoken prayers were answered
I am among all, most richly blessed.
Author Unknown

Epilogue

Road to Emmaus

$\mathscr{I}$have always found Luke Chapter 24: verses 13 to 35, the appearance on the road to Emmaus, to be very interesting. Jesus appears to and walks with two of His disciples who do not recognize Him. Wow! Either those guys are dumb as dirt or they have been drinking heavily! Yet it says in verse 16 "but their eyes were prevented from recognizing Him" Now why would Jesus do that? Is it because He is still "Rabboni", the teacher, and the lesson is He will no longer look the same as he abides in all of us. After His death and resurrection the gift of the Holy Spirit would be sent. In order to "see" Jesus we would have to look with the "eyes" of our heart. In 2nd Corinthians Chapter 6 verse 16 it says, "For we are the temple of the living God; as God said, 'I will be their God, and they shall be my people" Later back on the road to Emmaus, when the disciples invited the man walking with them to stay with them in Luke chapter 24 verses 30 32, it says,

> "And it happened that, while he was with them at table, he took bread, said the blessing, broke it, and gave it to them. With that their eyes were opened and they recognized him, but he vanished from their sight. Then they said to each other, 'Were not our hearts burning within us while he spoke to us on the way and opened the scriptures to us?'"

The blessing and the breaking of the bread represent the Eucharist and scripture is God's word. Through these means we will always be able to "see" Jesus clearly. It is how Jesus reveals Himself to us and it is the means by which we see Him in others.

Throughout my memoirs I expressed a desire to go to Medjugorje. On October 13th, 2000 I will be there. October 13th is the date of the last Fatima apparition and it is with great anticipation I await this trip. I look forward to praying in Saint James Church and giving thanks to Jesus and His Blessed Mother.

My Journey of Faith continues...

Poems and Letters

Choice

You chose darkness instead of light
You chose wrong instead of right
You chose personal gratification
Instead of religions sanctification
You chose this life and material things
Instead of the cross and the peace it brings
Still, if you wish, you can be saved
By following the way Jesus paved
It calls for conversion, a change of heart
But Heaven is yours when you depart
And into the arms of our Savior you go
Because in the end you reap what you sow.
- *Dawn Curazzato*

Divine Nature

Through the darkness comes the light
A morning dove's cry says farewell to night
A new day is dawning and with it comes hope
For those who are weary a reason to cope
The beauty of a new day often comes and goes
With no one taking notice of the lilac or rose
We take for granted life's beautiful things
The beauty and majesty each of them brings
How lucky the man who truly sees
The depth of life personified by trees
For he sees with the eyes of an open heart
And knows nature's tapestry as the Lord's work of art
And when darkness falls again on the land
The paintbrush of life stays in the Master's hand.
- *Dawn Curazzato*

The Son I Never Knew

When I ponder how I failed you
The happy times peek through
Little league and Disney world,
Trips made to the zoo
Now you're all grown up, the time just really flew
I seldom ever see you; our talks are far too few
I miss the little boy, who learned to tie his shoes,
Recite the alphabet and count for me by twos
I cry for the baby I gave birth to
And the bond that time unglued
But I do not cry for you
The son I never knew
I will always love you
That's what mothers do
Even for the son they never knew.
- *Dawn Curazzato*

Nightmare

It was dark
I was the mark
Someone is after me
A face I cannot see
My body has chills
Imagination kills
A shot from a gun
I start to run
I see a knife
The end of my life
Death is near
I'm paralyzed with fear
I scream
It's only a dream.
- Dawn Curazzato

Jesus

When the burdens of life bring you down
You need only call on Jesus
He will hear your cries and soothe your soul
And all of your pains He eases
When hopelessness comes
On the wings of despair
Call out the name of Jesus
And put all in His care
He comes with love and mercy
To do all He can to please us
He is love, He is our Savior
And His name is Jesus.
- Dawn Curazzato

Audrey Marie

Little Audrey with the long illustrious hair
Whom people visit in Faith and Prayer
God has given you gifts to appease us
To show us the way back to Jesus
Through your suffering God's graces extol
You are his purest victim soul
Before the Tabernacle day and night
Out of darkness and into the light
Your life is a prayer
To show God you care
For those who are sick you intercede
For conversion and forgiveness you also plead
Though you are silent, unable to talk
May the Lord will you, one day to walk
And when you awake may you be aware
Of all those who love you and keep you in prayer.
- Dawn Curazzato

Priest

A priest of the order of Melchizedek forever
The works of the Lord your life's endeavor
Your call puts you on the path to perfection
A life of prayer, sacrifice and reflection
Your homilies teach us about the Lord
That peace and faith may be restored
We hear about Genesis, the story of creation
Our Lord's death on the cross bringing us salvation
The stories of the apostles and the mark of the beast
All these things revealed through you, our Priest
Through songs and psalms with purposeful inflection
You lead your flock in Christ's direction
It is through you we come to know
As children of God we reap what we sow
Our Lord's commandments we are taught to obey
As well as the importance of prayer in our day
Through reconciliation it is our goal
To be free from sin and save our soul
You administer the Eucharist for us to receive
Body, Blood, Soul and Divinity, we believe!
In adoration we also give praise
For the happiness experienced in all of our days
When we open our hearts for the Lord to enter
And keep holy mass at the very center
We come to know Jesus is never very far
And we learn how dear our priests really are.
  - *Dawn Curazzato*

J.M.J.D.
AVE MARIA

Dominican Nuns of the Perpetual Rosary

Monastery of Our Lady of the Rosary
333 Doat St. – Buffalo, N.Y. 14211-2199

Aug. 11, 1997

Dear Mrs. Curazzato,

Thank you for your letter and for the wonderful attitude
you have toward the crosses in your life! Too often Christians
lose all their merit by complaining "Why me?". To say that so
many burdens are no burden uplifts us and must please God so
very much! Not many of His friends can be treated so severely
even though their faith should tell them that the cross is a
proof of God's Love, a splinter of Jesus' own Cross.

We shall indeed pray for you and for all your family, begging
for each the graces they need and a lifting of some of the suffering, God willing. We entrust all to the Immaculate Heart
of Mary and ask her help. If you can find time for a rosary
a day, this prayer will be a source of strength and comfort to
you and would be to your family members as well.

As for the M.S., your doctor could have told you that when
anyone developes it who is 40 or over they are not affected
as a younger person. The progress is very much slower and we
doubt that you have reason to worry about it. Too, we have
heard of a once a year injection for it that is very helpful.

In any case, God's Love surround you and your family and
He will take care of them even better than you can. But you
must trust Him completely. We pray you will be able to so trust,
even while we are praying that your health will hold out for
the years ahead.

Dominican Nuns of the Perpetual Rosary

International Compassion Ministry

Servite Fr. Peter M. Rookey, O.S.M.
20180 Governors Highway
Room 203
Olympia Fields, Illinois 60461-1067
(708) 748-MARY   Fax: (708) 748-0234

Sept. 3, 1997

Dear Dawn,

My heart goes out to you and your family in this time of suffering. One hour / day at a time, Dawn. Fear not the morrow. Fear paralyzes. Jesus I trust in you!

Jesus knows the needs of your family, Dawn. He will not abandon you. Remember all things work unto good for those who love the Lord.

Persevere in saying your rosary. Each bead of the rosary is a seed of faith, hope, and love. Pray it often and your spiritual garden will abound and yield all the graces you need.

You will be remembered along with all your family members in my daily Masses and prayers.

Love & prayers,

Peter Mary Rookey

J.M.J.D.
AVE MARIA

Dominican Nuns of the Perpetual Rosary

Monastery of Our Lady of the Rosary
333 Doat St. ~ Buffalo, N.Y. 14211-2199

DEC. 11, 1997

Dear Mrs. Curazzato,

May she who observed the first Advent help you pre-
pare your heart for the Birthday of her Divine Son! We
ask this grace for you with hearts grateful for your generous offering.

We are sorry to have taken so long to answer your letter but we put it aside to have more time when writing to
you. This season that time never comes!

We are so happy for you that you do not have M.S.! Be
sure of our continued prayers for your health. God will provide. As long as you are really needed you will be there for
your loved ones.

Katlin is one of God's special children whose mission in
this life (we all have one) is to suffer for others, just as
Jesus did. God's Love surrounds her in a special way so leave
her to One in charge. He is using the child. And one day He
will use you, perhaps to witness to the truth of Jesus' Presence in the Eucharist which so many no longer believe in.
We would be interested in knowing about the miracle when it
touches this devotion so dear to us who have Perpetual Adoration.

Gratefully in Jesus through Mary,

Dominican Nuns of the Perpetual Rosary

J.M.J.D.
AVE MARIA

Dominican Nuns of the Perpetual Rosary

Monastery of Our Lady of the Rosary
333 Doat St. ~ Buffalo, N.Y. 14211-2199

Feb. 27,1998

Dear Mrs. Curazzato,

     We are so happy for you–and for little Katelin! With
you we thank God and our Blessed Mother, while praying that
all will go well with her when the trache is taken out. Our
Lady does not do things by halves, so we know all will be
well and, God willing, get better and better. Its in reward
of your faith dear, and what you are trying to do for God
and His Mother.

     May They both reward you for your generous offering!
Be sure of our continued prayes for you and for all your family.

                Gratefully in Jesus through Mary,

                Dominican Nuns of the Perpetual Rosary

J.M.J.D.
AVE MARIA
Dominican Nuns of the Perpetual Rosary
Monastery of Our Lady of the Rosary
333 Doat St. ~ Buffalo, N.Y. 14211-2199

May 5,1999

Dear Mrs. Curazzato,

    May our lovely Queen of May bless you foryour offering. We are sincerely grateful forit and for a copy of the article, which we have posted. Some of the Sisters have followed Katelin's progress since you first wrote to us, with interest-and with the prayers of us all.

    The Lord is surely proving His special love for you-and testing your faith. Take one day, one hour, at a time for that is all we ever have grace for. We can't carry to-morrow's cross until it comes. When it comes, the grace to carry it will come with it. That attitude will keep you from being scared, which is natural enough. But living for the present moment is a good way to avoid unnecessary suffering-which "crossing bridges" ahead of time always brings with it. You have done more for God's glory in the past 3 years than the average person would do in several lifetimes! He will not abandon you now!

    We will be praying for your daughter's safe delivery and for you. In fact you are all wrapped up in our rosaries! And we are sure our Blessed Mother has her arms around you, for every mother wants to be near a suffering child.How much morethis best of Mothers!

            Gratefully in Her,
            Dominican Nuns of thePerpetual Rosary

About the Author

Mrs. Dawn Curazzato along with her husband, Sam, have two children, Lisa and Joe as well as three grandchildren, Shane, Katelin and Connor. Her love and devotion to her family is paramount and reflects her great love and trust in God and His church

Katelin's miracle has been reported on television in a News Special, on Unsolved Mysteries and in a lengthy article in the Western New York Catholic Newspaper. It is also recorded in this book and in the hearts of all who know her.

Though the contents deal with private revelation, the author affirms her unconditional submission to the final judgment of the church

Printed in the United States
209438BV00002B/154-165/A